"I smiled, chortled, and laughed out loud. This book is hilarious. Jack has a wonderful ability to turn the seemingly mundane into truly entertaining prose. I love how some of the humour builds—from kernel to crescendo—while at other moments, it hits on the blindside, provoking a sudden spit-your-coffee-out snort of laughter."

SUSAN LUNDY award-winning journalist and author of *Home on the Strange: Chronicles of Motherhood, Mayhem and Matters of the Heart*

"Jack Knox brings his *Fortune Knox Once* to our table like everyone's fun uncle who shows up and makes us feel better. He spins a merry web around the absurdity of our lives lately and it's a relief to giggle and know we're all in this together!"

LESLEY CREWE bestselling author of *I Kid You Not: Chronicles of an Ordinary Family*

FORTUNE KNOX ONCE

MORE MUSINGS FROM THE EDGE

Jack Knox

JACK KNOX

HERITAGE

Heritage House Publishing Company Ltd.
heritagehouse.ca

Cataloguing information available from Library and Archives Canada

978-1-77203-417-2 (*paperback*)
978-1-77203-418-9 (*e-book*)

Edited by Lesley Cameron
Cover design by Setareh Ashrafologhalai and Jacqui Thomas
Interior book design by Jacqui Thomas

The interior of this book was produced on 100% post-consumer
recycled paper, processed chlorine free, and printed
with vegetable-based inks.

Heritage House gratefully acknowledges that the land on which
we live and work is within the traditional territories of the Lkwungen
(Esquimalt and Songhees), Malahat, Pacheedaht, Scia'new, T'Sou-ke,
and W̲SÁNEĆ (Pauquachin, Tsartlip, Tsawout, Tseycum) Peoples.

We acknowledge the financial support of the Government of Canada
through the Canada Book Fund (CBF) and the Canada Council
for the Arts, and the Province of British Columbia through the
British Columbia Arts Council and the Book Publishing Tax Credit.

26 25 24 23 22 1 2 3 4 5

Printed in Canada

To all the ink-stained wretches

Table of  Contents

Introduction

ONE LONG-AGO NIGHT, I had the flu. So did my wife. So did our infant, who, while writhing in 3:00 AM discomfort, managed to head butt me in the face, splitting my lip.

At that point it seemed like a good idea (at least to me) to exit the living room and hand off the child to my wife, which I did. Then—nauseated, sleep-deprived, and bleeding from the mouth—I staggered back to the bedroom, flopped down on the mattress, and thought, "What's next?"

That's when I heard the dog barfing in the hallway.

And that, dear reader, is the past few years in a nutshell.

Really, it has been one thing after another. So far, this decade has been like the opening to an Indiana Jones movie, hurling us from one crisis to the next until, breathless and dazed, we found ourselves reeling in circles, fedoras askew, masks riding up over our eyes, waiting for a giant rolling boulder to crush us to death. By now we could all use a laugh.

That's all this book tries to do: give you a reason to smile. It won't change your life. It won't give you deep insight into the human condition. It won't offer Ten Steps to Unlocking Your Inner You! or whatever. It might make it easier to drift off to sleep (don't read it while driving).

Its working title was *Island Idiot* because that's who I am: a garden-variety doofus who has spent most of his adult life on Vancouver Island, slightly detached from reality, or at least the rest of Canada. Much of the writing that follows is from the per-spective of (and pokes a bit of fun at) the Island and Victoria, though you don't have to live in Dysfunction-By-The-Sea to get the humour. Much of it falls into the category of social commen-tary. Or unmitigated piffle. Take your pick.

Fortune Knox Once is similar to my previous books in that it is based largely on my columns in the Victoria *Times Colonist* newspaper, albeit tweaked, updated, and smooshed together where appropriate. If you read and enjoyed *Hard Knox* or *Opportunity Knox*, you'll probably enjoy *Fortune Knox Once* too. (If you didn't enjoy those books, I would suggest giving this one to someone you loathe.)

The subject matter is all over the map: the lost art of handwriting, the sexiness of the Canadian accent, phone addiction, the Rogue Cow of Metchosin, ugly trucks, ugly people, a parody of end-of-school announcements and a letter to Prince Harry. There's a piece on Canada's growing waste problem and another on the problem of Canada's growing waists. Wait until you get to the chapter on Pi Day; it's possibly some of the best math-based humour you'll read all week.

I'm not going to dwell on the pandemic in these pages. COVID-19 is like the Trump era, impossible to ignore but we're all tired of talking about it, even if it was a gold mine for humour. I group together a dozen pieces on plague-related topics—the dog shortage, doomscrolling, the time I dropped my credit card into the saltchuck—in a section called Two Years Before the Mask, but otherwise the coronavirus appears only in brief glimpses, like a moustache-twirling villain occasionally creeping onto the stage in an old-style British pantomime.

I rant a bit in places, because doing so always makes me feel better. I also engage in the odd flight of fancy. My old pal Buck the urban deer wanders into the book in a couple of places, leaving muddy hoofprints on the pages as usual. (Deer are pigs.) So does Jesus Christ, hiding backstage at a school concert. So does a fictitious version of my wife. People ask me if she's actually the unsympathetic character I sometimes portray her to be. No, I reply, she's much, much worse. Really, just awful, but please don't tell her I said so.

Also included are a couple of stories about people whose lives and deaths might make you feel sad and good at the same time. Those stories aren't humour pieces, but it isn't always humour that makes us smile.

Anyway, I hope you enjoy *Fortune Knox Once* as much as I've enjoyed my own good fortune. I've been in a privileged position for a long time, for which I am—seriously—profoundly grateful.

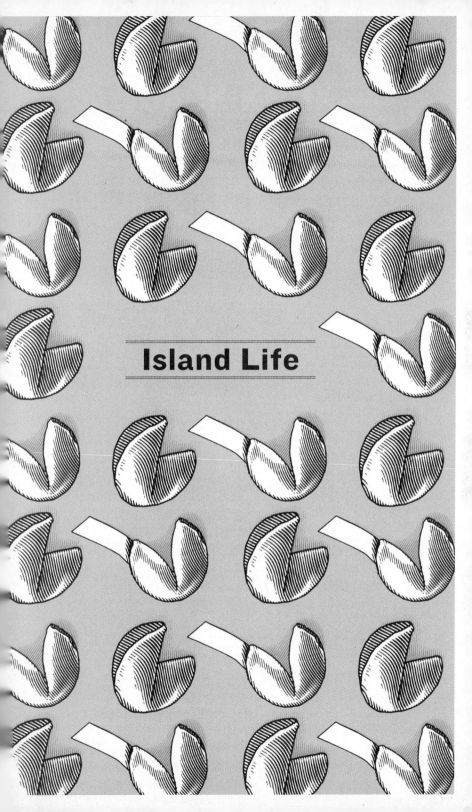

Island Life

Stepping Back

N EARLY 2020, AFTER spending the holidays near Victoria, the Duke and Duchess of Sussex—otherwise known as Harry and Meghan—briefly flirted with the idea of putting down roots on Vancouver Island. I tried to encourage them with the following letter.

Dear Prince Harry,

May I call you Prince? Probably not. You're not a golden retriever.

Sorry, this is new territory for us. If your just-finished North Saanich holiday left us unfazed, the news that you might be relocating here semi-permanently sent us into a flutter. ("You polish the corgis," I told the missus. "I'll hide the empty beer cans under the porch.")

We don't even know how (or whether) to greet you should we end up in line together at the Sidney Bakery. Curtsy? Fist bump? Probably best to avoid repeating that episode where Mr. Bean head-butted the Queen while trying to bow.

Speaking of your grandmother, we understand she's miffed about your decision to "step back" from the family firm and spend more time on this side of the pond.

Never mind. Stories such as yours are common here. Should you move to Vancouver Island, you will find no shortage of people who, despite the little choking noises emitted by their families, chose to "step back" from medical school/Bay Street/the Vietnam War in favour of a promising career in batik-based fashion at the Salt Spring market, or whatever.

In fact, making a conscious decision to jump off the escalator is pretty much a prerequisite for relocating to our edge-of-the-world paradise. If you want to rocket to the top, go to Toronto, the centre of the (Canadian) universe. If you want to pick a bucket of blackberries, come here. For all the rah-rah of those who want to portray Victoria as a high-energy, high-tech hub packed with people rushing around in suits so hip and stylish that they appear to have been made for a slightly smaller man, to most of us it's still a provincial backwater, tucked away in an out-of-the-way corner of Canada like the forgotten spare tire for a car you no longer own. That's its greatest attraction.

This is a place for those who come from somewhere else in search of something else. History has brought them to Vancouver Island in waves: Spanish explorers, British traders, Chinese labourers, California gold miners, Finnish Utopians, '60s dropouts, American refugees escaping the madness. Gulf Islands thrift stores glitter with the designer labels and power suits that their owners have shed in favour of Gore-Tex and gumboots.

True, as an outsider, you will at first have many questions about your new home:

"Why do we have pints of beer but litres of gas?"

"Why does no one own a snow shovel, even though it snows every year?"

"What is a two-sailing wait, and why should I be upset about it?"

"Why is Ice Road Truckers on the History Channel?"

Don't worry. You won't take long to fit in. Just as no one waves a maple leaf flag as vigorously as an immigrant does (more than one in five Canadians were born outside Canada, BTW), no one embraces the Island lifestyle as passionately as those who opted to come here from elsewhere. After a year, you'll think the

Royals are a hockey team. After two, you'll eat kale on purpose and think the Greens have a chance of forming a government.

Now, perhaps I'm getting ahead of myself. To be honest, there is little evidence, aside from the game of Where's Waldo/Meghan currently playing out on the Saanich Peninsula, that you plan to replant yourselves on Vancouver Island at all. There is a solid case to be made for making this your North American base, though. It's safe, secluded, and leafy; it enjoys a moderate climate; it's part of the Commonwealth; and, best of all, it's 7,662 kilometres from the kind of unrelenting, invasive scrutiny from which anyone would want to shield those they love.

Jeez, if you needed validation that you made the right choice in fleeing the circus, just look at the reaction you've been getting from the clowns since making your announcement. Even as an ardent monarchist (I can tolerate Canadian republicans; it's not their fault they're totally dead inside), I am aghast at the vicious treatment you have been getting from British royalists. We haven't seen their kind of over-the-top, bile-spitting indignation since Victoria began building bike lanes. You'd think you were defecting to North Korea, not bunking in North Saanich. Yet they wonder why you would want to come here, far from the baying hounds.

Anyway, welcome. You'll fit right in among the rest of the people who decided to "step back" into the life they want.

Settling for Silver

NEWS ITEM: Victoria is the second-best
small city in the world.

—*Condé Nast* Readers' Choice awards

I **CONFRONTED HER AS SHE** got off the plane in Victoria: "So,
who is this guy?" Startled, she dropped her carry-on bag. The
sound of breaking glass was followed by the pungent smell of
tequila. "Wh . . . who?" she stammered.

"Miguel!" I replied. I knew his name but had never seen
him. Sexy Latin lover, all flashing white teeth and smouldering
eyes, I imagined.

"Who?" she repeated, but she couldn't meet my gaze.

"San Miguel de Allende," I spat. This time she didn't even
bother with a denial.

"What's he got that we don't have?" I demanded. "Cheap
ferry fares? Regional transportation planning? On-time bridge
construction?"

"He's just so . . . so hot," the woman admitted with a sigh.

Couldn't deny that. San Miguel de Allende was 26°C on
Wednesday. Much nicer than the wind-whipped soaking here in
Gloomy-by-the-Water.

Maybe that's why the readers of *Condé Nast Traveler* rated
the Mexican community one spot ahead of Victoria when rating
the best small cities outside the US.

Now, some tourist towns would be happy with second place.
Look at the destinations ranked below Victoria in the small-cities
placings: Florence, Bruges, Lucerne, Salzburg, Edinburgh,
Stockholm, Prague . . . Most cities would be happy to wallow at
the bottom of that list, let alone nudge the top. Not Victoria.

Others might be content with the silver medal. Here, we take it as an affront.

Victoria is used to being No. 1.

To repeat: Various studies have declared this to be the smartest, most desirable, most romantic city in Canada. It is also, according to the Canadian Centre for Policy Alternatives, the best city in which to be a woman. I assumed this last finding might have something to do with the magnificence* of the typical Victoria chick magnet (*paunchy, grey-haired, grey-skinned, yellow-toothed, self-absorbed, vaguely redolent of weed), but no, no, the study said it was due largely to Victoria being the only one of twenty-five cities where more women than men are employed, and where they make up almost half of all senior managers and elected officials.

Not that we need the external validation. Vancouver might go to DEFCON 3 every time some B-list celebrity says something slightly derogatory (note that when *Riverdale* star K.J. Apa dubbed the city "kind of boring" in 2017, it triggered the kind of confidence crisis not seen since *The X-Files'* David Duchovny complained about the rain in 1997), but self-confident Victoria doesn't question itself in that way.

Still, when people say we should be happy about being second-best after San Miguel de Allende, that's like telling Sidney Crosby he should be happy being second to Connor McDavid.

"Why would you rather visit him than us?" I demanded of the woman at the airport. "What's he got that we don't?"

This time she stared at me defiantly. "Designation as a World Heritage Site. A historic town centre crammed with baroque Spanish architecture from the seventeenth and eighteenth centuries. A Gothic church whose striking pink spires soar over the cobblestoned streets below."

This changed my image of Miguel. Obviously, she had fallen for an older man.

"OK," I said, "but we offer one hour free in select municipal parkades." Then I mimed a mic drop and walked away.

She called after me: "It's his relaxed atmosphere, his languid pace."

I wheeled on her. "You want slow-paced? Try the commute from the West Shore when it's raining, baby. Or the Malahat on a summer Sunday. Or getting a building permit for anything over three storeys in Cook Street Village."

I saw no need to mention two-sailing waits for the ferries, two-year waits for surgery, or our, um, measured approach to municipal decision-making. (Why does it take so long to get anything done in Victoria? Because we spend so much time staring at the mirror, reflecting on our total awesomeness.)

Nor was it necessary to bring up our other advantages. Sure, San Miguel might have a vibrant arts scene, but does it offer an excellent selection of thirteen boutique micro-governments, each with its own eclectic and inventive approach to bike lanes, speed limits, policing, pot shops, garbage disposal, and snow removal? A quick glance at the brochure shows no hint of a North Miguel, Central Miguel, Miguel-By-The-Sea, or Miguelford. Losers.

Also, you have to give the edge to our nightlife. That is, we don't have any. Frankly, it's a relief to pull on our slippers at the same time the Mexicans are squeezing into their dancing shoes. (A Food Network host once theorized that Victoria's brunch scene is so hot because nobody stays up late enough for supper. That, and we all have night blindness so are afraid to drive to the restaurants.)

We might be second to Condé Nast, but we're first to bed.

Don't Poke the Moose

NEWS ITEM: Victoria's downtown business association removes posters reading "Chill, we could all be in Moose Jaw" after the Saskatchewan city takes offence.

The signs were part of a campaign urging grumbling Victorians to lighten up about parking problems in the city's core.

ON BEHALF OF VICTORIA, I wish to apologize to Moose Jaw from the bottom of my heart, or at least the heart of my bottom.

When we poked fun at you with those downtown parking posters, we didn't mean to single out Moose Jaw as a bleak, frostbitten, featureless place to live. No, no, no. What you have to understand is that by "Moose Jaw" we meant "all of Saskatchewan." And by "Saskatchewan," we mean "everywhere on the wrong side of the Rockies." In fact, we also look down our noses at Vancouver, Kelowna, Prince George (the city, not the child)—all of Eastern Canada, really, which we define as anything past Tsawwassen. It's why we dug the big moat between us and them: to keep the riff-raff out.

For we in Victoria believe we live in the most special place in Canada, if not all of creation. Retirees flock here. So do tourists. There are angels in Heaven who dream of buying a house on Ten Mile Point. We tell each other this—modestly, repeatedly, and loudly—while burning our overdue-mortgage-payment notices to stay warm in the homes we can't afford to heat. (Ha ha! Those stupid Moose Jaw people, underpaying for their houses, having to figure out what to do with all that extra disposable income.)

Regrettably, in poking fun at Moose Jaw, we broke a cardinal rule: The prettiest girl at the dance is not supposed to acknowledge that she is the prettiest girl. And certainly, when told she's a rotten dancer or she has lousy parking skills, she isn't supposed to respond with "Chill, you could be dancing with that girl with the funny name." It's bad manners.

Not only that, but it risks creating resentment. (Echoes of Kelly LeBrock's 1980s shampoo commercial: "Don't hate me because I'm beautiful.") While the rest of Canada knows Victoria is lovely, that doesn't mean they have to love Victorians. (Remember when the city got buried in the Blizzard of '96? Alberta declared a civic holiday.) If we tick off the rest of the country, the rest of the country is likely to key our car after the dance or force a pipeline to our coast.

As it is, other Canadians are not as smitten with us as we are with ourselves. Victoria might think of itself as a beautiful princess, but others see a tinfoil hat where the tiara is supposed to be. For this is how others view us: Old-World stuffy or hipster pretentious one moment, chemtrails-crazy the next.

That's the prevailing view of BC in general. As one of two token British Columbians working in the newsroom of the *Regina Leader Post* in the 1980s, half my time was spent trying to dispel the notion that our province was nothing but a refuge for burned-out acid heads and edge-of-the-world crackpots, the place where the rest of Canada shovelled its flakes in winter.

Alas, as I was self-righteously bleating in our defence one day, the newswire spat out Keith Baldrey's *Vancouver Sun* story about a chaotic confrontation between fundamentalist Christians and a ragtag collection of protesters—including

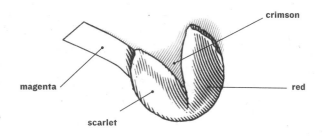

crimson

magenta

red

scarlet

enviros, pagans, and a Sufi—who invaded the new prayer room at the BC legislature. ("Tolerance is ignorance," bellowed a fundamentalist as a variety of gods were invoked to, among other things, fight uranium mining. "I heard something about Buddha here, and I didn't like it.") Basically, just another day at the circus.

After that, no one in Regina took me seriously, though one guy did keep sidling up to quietly ask if I knew where he could buy some mushrooms.

It was also in Regina that my wife met a cab driver who had once lived in Vancouver. He explained what brought him back to Saskatchewan: "I got up one morning, looked at those damned mountains on one side and that ruddy ocean on the other, and said: 'I've got to go home.'" Home being where the heart is—and if you poke fun at somebody's home, don't be surprised if they poke you back.

Honk If You Love Road Rage

AUGUST. DOWNTOWN. RUSH HOUR.
Hot pavement, hotter drivers, the smoke from their ears mixing with the exhaust from their tailpipes as they inch along. Yet another construction project has funnelled two lanes into one, and the funnel is full.

A little drama is playing out at the squeeze point. A man has glided up the relatively empty right-hand lane and now wants into the left, but the woman in the left isn't having it, not after having been stuck in line through two light changes. She's hanging onto the car in front like it's the last chopper out of Saigon in '75, so close you couldn't slip a credit card between their bumpers. No way she's letting buddy in the right lane butt in—except he forces his way in anyway.

This is when something unbelievable happens: The first driver leans on her horn.

For real. In Victoria. A horn honk just like in the movies.

This has the effect you might expect: The world comes to a sudden halt. Birds stop singing. Pedestrians turn and gape. Some, uncertain where the jarring sound came from, look aloft. One driver, suspecting catastrophic engine failure, gets out and peers under his hood.

This being Victoria, several among the gathering crowd blame the strange noise on A) chemtrails, B) the vaccine, C) an acid flashback, or D) the mayor.

"No," says a young woman, a recent visitor to Toronto, "that was a car horn."

There's an audible gasp, followed by a muffled scream. Several onlookers make the sign of the cross. Two of them faint.

One does not sound one's horn in Victoria, at least not in anger. It's just not done. To employ a horn as some sort of audible middle finger is considered an act of violence. Might as well empty a Glock through the back window or wear white after Labour Day. We treat the horns in our cars in the same way hormonal teenage boys carry condoms in their wallets—neither expecting nor knowing how to use them.

Except now, apparently, we do. Same day as the downtown beeping, I saw—or heard—somebody blare his horn after almost becoming the victim of another driver's ill-timed turn on Cadboro Bay Road. Then, same day again, someone else played an extended one-note lament while inching down coagulated Wharf Street.

This is the way horns are most often used. The law says we're only supposed to sound them to warn other drivers of impending danger, but mostly we do it to express frustration or scold others.

Most jurisdictions have rules that ban such gratuitous honking, though they're seldom enforced. Some drivers do get charged, though: In the US, offenders have argued their honking constitutes an act of protest and should therefore be protected as free speech. Not so, the courts have ruled.

Also, history shows that if you do use your horn as an alternative to slugging another driver in the nose, chances are you'll get punched on your own honker.

Not long ago, a Calgary man whose horn-honking escalated into race-based abuse was charged with a hate crime. Soon after, a Washington state hornfest ended with a shirtless man (always a sign of stability) throwing an axe at another driver's window. More recently, a Michigan man pulled a gun on a vehicle carrying eight children after the latter vehicle's driver honked at him for not moving at a green light. In Tennessee, a woman who sounded her horn after being cut off in traffic was shot at by a woman in the offending car. Honking made No. 6 on CBS News's "Road Rage: Nine Ways to Get Yourself Killed" list.

None of this explains why we hear horns more often these days, though. Is it the pandemic? The early days of COVID-19 actually ushered in an era of positive horn use, with drive-by parades of vehicles substituting for in-person grad ceremonies, birthday parties, and baby showers. Now, though, the honking reflects frayed tempers or anxiety or a lashing-out against all we've had to deal with. Note that when Victoria was invaded by flag-draped convoys of pandemic protesters, they leaned on their horns as a substitute for presenting a rational argument.

I have my own honking story: Many years ago, shortly after news anchor Hudson Mack jumped from CHEK to what was then known as "A" Channel, he found himself at the wheel of his new station's float as it approached the platform from which CHEK broadcast the Victoria Day parade. Not wanting to show its rival, CHEK swung a camera away from the parade and onto me: "Hey, Jack, tell us what's coming up in the *Times Colonist* . . ." As I stammered a reply, Mack stopped the float in the middle of Douglas Street and leaned on the horn to drown out my answer, all the while grinning demonically at me over the cameraman's shoulder. It was hard not to laugh.

But I digress. Irate honking has no place in civilized society, or even Alberta. Give in to that temptation and next thing you know we'll be living a lawless, dystopian nightmare where roving gangs of feral youth loot liquor stores and drivers budge into ferry-terminal line-ups with impunity.

Think in terms of texting, with the horn as a send button, never to be pushed when angry.

Fun(?) Run

IT'S THE *TIMES COLONIST* 10K fun run today. A friend of mine has dreams of finishing in less than forty minutes.

I, too, hope to break forty this morning—forty winks, that is. Yes, when 10,000 fit, eager entrants crowd the start line by the Inner Harbour, I will be among a record 840,000 Islanders not running this year's race. I'll be dreaming of finishing nothing more demanding than a plate of bacon and eggs.

With luck, I won't get out of bed until the first racers stagger across the finish line, sometime around 8:30 AM. That would shatter my current personal record, 8:15.

I am, in fact, going for the double: Not only am I not running the TC10K today, I'm not running the 10-kilometre Sun Run in Vancouver either. Some people think not running two races back-to-back like that is overdoing it, but as I like to say, "Reach for the stars, or maybe just another cup of coffee."

I actually toyed with the idea of signing up for the race at the last minute, but abandoned the notion because A) I have a conveniently wonky knee, B) I have to wash my hair, and C) I haven't run with any sense of purpose since 1981, when a biker pulled a knife on me in Amsterdam. I am not a runner. I come from a long line of non-runners. My great-uncle Augustus, the one who died bravely at Vimy Ridge? Wasn't brave at all. Just slow.

On those occasions when I do enter the TC10K, I make sure to drift back to the Big Underwear section, where the participants tend to show up with packs of smokes rolled into the sleeves of their souvenir T-shirts and prefer to compete in bedroom slippers, not athletic shoes. I like to amble sedately through the race course, only breaking into a trot when in sight of the finish line, a camera, or a good-looking woman. If you are a woman and see me running, take it as a compliment. In truth, I have always loathed running, despising it more than Hitler, quinoa, and the 1975 Philadelphia Flyers all rolled into one. If you are a man and see me running, then you should run too, because it's a sure bet that something truly threatening is close behind.

My wife, on the other hand, runs a lot—10Ks, half-marathons, marathons, and even ultra-marathons. Sometimes I cheer her on, standing on the side of the road and calling out, "What's for supper" or "Can't you go faster? I'm getting bored." She's always happy to see me when she crosses the finish line, blurting out, "Oh my God, I can't shake him," and bursting into tears of joy.

It was she who persuaded me to sign up for a TC10K running clinic one year. I'd like to think she did so out of concern for my health, but I suspect it had more to do with sadistic curiosity. I still don't know what drove me to go along with her idea. Must have been the heady euphoria brought on by achieving a personal best at the previous year's race. Never mind that my personal best was still slightly slower than the federal bureaucracy.

Anyway, my running clinic turned out to be fourteen weeks (or, as I called it, fifty years) long. Participants chose programs that matched their level of ability, sorting themselves into groups with names like First Steps, Next Steps, and Running Well. I believe I was in my clinic's Learn to Barf section. After the first session, I figured I should skip the clinic and go straight to the hospital.

Still, much to my surprise, my ordeal eventually turned out to be fun (though I may be confusing "fun" with "oxygen deprivation"). The volunteer leaders were all upbeat and positive and would say supportive things like "You're looking great," and "Remember to keep your head up," and "I don't think he's breathing, maybe we should call an ambulance." My fellow trainees were encouraging too. ("Ten kilometres? You'll be fine. It'll fly by like three movies.")

My wife also helped. "Let me pin your registration number on your back," she said. Only it wasn't my registration number, was it? It was a sign that read "Free to a good home."

"Just kidding," she said. "It doesn't have to be a good home. Look at all the women here. There must be one who would take you. I'll throw in a toaster oven too."

Anyway, when I crossed the finish line at the 10K, they all cheered as though I had edged out Usain Bolt, not an eighty-year-old man recovering from a stroke.

That still didn't make me a runner, though. Even going downhill, I looked like an unmade bed that had tumbled out the back of a moving van. Snails gave me the finger as they roared past. But it's all relative, isn't it? A while ago, I saw Bruce Deacon, Olympian and three-time TC10K winner, run by. He was really moving. "How are you doing?" Bruce said. The "how are" came out when he was half a block behind me, the "you" when we were parallel, and the "doing" was pretty much all Doppler effect, the sound hanging around a split second longer than Bruce, who was gone faster than an election promise, leaving nothing but a Matrix-like ripple of air in his wake.

And that's when I stopped thinking "everybody is faster than me" and started thinking "almost everybody is slower than Bruce," which made me feel better. No point worrying about anyone other than yourself. To all those lacing up this morning, enjoy the day. That's why they call it a fun run (which is, of course, an oxymoron).

Gas Pains

I RECORDED A NEW PERSONAL best today.

It was a bit of a surprise. I thought it might happen on the day of the next *Times Colonist* 10K race, but no, no, it looks like my peak came early.

I had to drain the tank to do it, mind you. Drove myself to the limit, was running on fumes. My reward? The numbers at the end.

"It's my first $60 fill-up," I told the gas station attendant, shoving my credit card across the counter. I tried to look modest, but couldn't stop grinning as the clerk (who did a better job than I at feigning a lack of interest) rejected the card and passed back a loan application instead.

I was giddy. Sure, I had come close before—there was that time when pandemic travel restrictions eased and Victoria gas hit $1.53 a litre—but even then I couldn't quite make the pump click past $59.99. It wasn't until today, with the price topping $2, that I was able to burn a couple of celebratory smoking-tire NASCAR victory laps around the lot.

It helped, of course, that gas prices jumped more than a dime in a day. Why? They always have a reason. A refinery is down, or crude is up. Or a pipeline is out of commission. Or Alberta is throwing another hissy fit. Or the Washington state refineries are charging us a premium because, well, if we don't like it, they'll just sell their gas to California instead. They have us over a barrel (as it were). I'd like to thank them all.

Now, I know what you're saying: Jack, if you really wanted to shatter the magic $60 barrier, why didn't you buy a less fuel-efficient car? Some vehicles suck sixty bucks' worth just idling in the drive-through on the way to Earth Day.

Oddly enough, these vehicles are often driven by the same people who moan the loudest about high gas prices. People who don't really have to drive something the size of your first apartment. Some people—farmers, builders, Mad Max—might need a rig that big, but it's not like the rest of us are going to have to clear a rock slide or winch cattle out of the slough while four-wheeling downtown.

No matter what we drive, we react to every gas price jump as though we A) didn't see it coming and B) can't believe Big Oil is getting away with it.

Alas, it's like being kicked in the crotch by the school bully. First time it happened, in the 1970s, we were shocked, spitting with indignation. We went to the principal and said, "Mr. Trudeau, Big Oil just kicked me in the crotch."

Then it happened again—oof!—and frankly, it wasn't any less shocking the second time around, so we went: "Mr. Mulroney, Big Oil just did it again."

After the third time ("Mr. Chrétien!"), the shock (though not the sensation) was beginning to wear off, and by the fourth ("Oh, jeez, Mr. Harper"), we had pretty much figured out that, fair or not, getting booted in the nether regions was an occasional fact of life, so we might as well protect ourselves, preferably with something with airbags in front.

Some people adapt. It's easy to identify them, because they'll tell you about it, over and over. "I get 140 kilometres to the litre of canola oil," they say, poking their heads out of what appears to be a bread maker on wheels. "I charge my car with excess power from my vacuum cleaner. Also, I heat my home with tidal power from the bathtub and play canasta with Elizabeth May on Wednesday nights. Can I borrow your truck? I have to go to the dump."

Of course, we could cut down on driving altogether—going by bus, or walking, or cycling, or carpooling—but that's not what's happening. The number of insured vehicles on Vancouver Island keeps rising, and no, most aren't electric. Apparently, fuel prices aren't that high after all, at least not yet.

They say gas could reach a new record this summer, though. I feel another personal best coming on.

Chasing the Almighty Buck

DROVE UP TO MY supposedly empty house, only to find the front door wide open.

Burglar? No. I should be so lucky.

I sighed. "What are you doing here, Buck?"

Slumped in a living room chair—my chair—Buck ignored my question. Instead, poking at an iPad with his front hooves, he asked one of his own: "What's our Wi-Fi password?"

"Define 'our,'" I replied. "And is that a tomato plant hanging from your antlers?" That question was rhetorical. I knew what I'd find in the garden. Sure enough, the tomatoes were toast. Ditto for the—damn him!—almost-ripe peas. The flower beds were just beds. Deer have a rather elastic respect for private property.

Buck at least had the good grace to look sheepish. "Sorry," he said. "I was famished after work."

Work? "I'm a tester at a pot farm," he said. "We're slammed right now. Second-quarter numbers are going to be through the roof. I barely have time for yoga in the morning. Just hit the Starbucks drive-through and go."

Well, it was inevitable, wasn't it? Our old friend Buck the Deer has turned into a fully fledged city boy. And so have his friends.

It was about thirty years ago that deer first became noticeable in the city, tiptoeing gingerly out of the forest before timidly nipping the heads off the odd Gordon Head tulip. A generation later, they had become bold enough to chase dogs and shrug at golf-course duffers. Today, Victoria's black-tails are fully urban animals, avoiding eye contact with panhandlers, brazenly chewing through the produce while "shopping" at the grocery store, doing the head-bob crotch-check thing while pretending not to text at red lights.

And they've lost their fear of humans. One day, I came across Buck slouched against an Oak Bay Avenue storefront doing his best James Dean: Black leather jacket, toothpick dangling from his lips, rat-tail comb stuck in his hindquarter. The biker cap jammed between his antlers just looked silly, though. Also, his hooves didn't have enough knuckles for the traditional L-O-V-E H-A-T-E tattoo, so it came out L-O H-A, which was more Hawaiian than hostile.

"I'm being aggressive," Buck explained.

"I know," I said. "You charged at Gregor Craigie. Why him? Everybody likes Gregor."

"That was the point," Buck replied. "I was sending a message: Nobody's safe. It's like mugging Tom Hanks."

OK, maybe it wasn't actually Buck who did it, but CBC Radio host Craigie really did have a deer stalker, as it were. He was walking through Oak Bay with his fifteen-year-old husky-cross Nanuk tightly leashed at his side when, without warning, a snorting deer came charging across a lawn, precipitating a slow-speed but persistent chase in which the angry ungulate followed man and dog as they circled a parked car. Round and round they went, just like the pipeline debate, with the deer giving Craigie the Travis Bickle "You talkin' to me?" death stare until they all got dizzy and staggered off in different directions.

Stories like this should no longer surprise us. More deer live on the edges of our cities now than in the heart of the forest. Other animals have migrated too. *Popular Science* says coyotes use traffic lights to negotiate the streets of downtown Chicago, and that foxes have colonized London, England—one was even found on the seventy-second floor of an unfinished skyscraper, where it survived on construction workers' lunch scraps.

In *National Geographic* magazine, the Dutch evolutionary biologist Menno Schilthuizen spoke of the speed with which animals adapt to cities: Mosquitoes found in different London

Underground lines are genetically distinct from one another, as are bobcats on different sides of a Los Angeles freeway. Crows in Japan have learned to crack walnuts by dropping them in front of slow-moving vehicles. Aided by big-city lights, traditionally diurnal birds have become night hunters.

Given their history of adaptation, we all know what's next for our urban deer: the rat race. Sure, it's nice to have an all-you-can-eat buffet in every back yard, but that lifestyle comes with a cost—heavy traffic, pollution, congestion, noise. Then there's job pressure, property taxes, car insurance ... Save up for a little place in the country, somewhere to get away from it all, only to spend every evening and weekend working overtime to pay for the mortgage. And just when you think you're in clover, the roof leaks or the water heater goes or the transmission seizes and you're back at it, not so much a stag in the wild as a hamster on a wheel—the mighty Buck chasing the almighty buck.

A Love That Never Died

YES, THIS IS A humour book, but let's pause a moment for a love story.

It began in 1957, at the Hong Kong shipping company where Chan Yung Tong and Katima Amy Ismail both worked.

It continued long after her death, on the mornings, close to six thousand of them, when Chan caned his way up the hill to Saanich's Royal Oak Burial Park on his daily journey to her grave. And it continued until the end of 2019, when he was laid to rest in the plot next to hers, right where he wanted to be.

Katima was born in 1927, descended from a man who went to Hong Kong from India with the British army during the opium wars of the nineteenth century. Chan—he wrote his name in the Chinese fashion, surname first—was a Hong Kong native too. She was the big boss's secretary at the shipping company, whereas he toiled further down the corporate food chain. It wasn't love at first sight ("I don't chase her. She don't chase me," he would later say).

One day, Chan looked at the entertainment ads in the newspaper and said he wanted to see a movie. She said she wanted to see it too. He got the Hong Kong Regiment discount, paying $1.70 for his ticket, while hers cost $2.40. She was a tad surprised when he asked her for the $2.40.

They began to see each other more and more after that, going for coffee, that sort of thing. Still, it was months before they even held hands. Then, one day, while trying to negotiate a slippery sidewalk, she took his arm. They were married on March 11, 1959.

In the beginning, her family wanted him to embrace Islam, but it never really took, at least not then. Giving up pork was his big concession to her religion. "Even chow mein, always beef or chicken, never pork," he said. His family says it was only in the last year or two of his life that he fully converted, believing it would give him a better chance of being with Katima in the afterlife.

If complications from surgery left her unable to conceive, being childless also left the couple free to travel, which they did extensively: Asia, Europe, and three trips to Victoria, where Chan had a younger sister. He wanted to move to Vancouver Island, but Katima wasn't as keen. "My wife doesn't like. Too cold," he explained. A sundrenched trip to Expo '86 tipped the scales, though. They settled in Victoria officially in 1988.

It was a good life, a good love, the kind that doesn't need a lot of talking. "Silly man," she called him. Some couples drift apart, but they just grew closer. "Even now, I'm more and more in love," he said one day, eight years after her death.

The irony, considering the strength of their love, is that it was her heart that weakened. Chan would take the bus to Royal Jubilee Hospital every day, catching the final run back to Esquimalt at night. For the last couple of weeks of her life, he was allowed to use the bed next to hers. Chan would ask her, "You hate me?" She would shake her head, no. "You love me?" A nod, yes.

She knew she was slipping away, told him Muslims don't cry at the time of death. "But I cannot stop," Chan said. Katima died on October 6, 2001. "I hold her hand, and the heart stop."

It was then that Chan began the daily journeys he promised her he would make. Up at 5:15 AM, out the door in time for the 7:30 bus to the burial park. Sometimes he brought carnations. Sometimes he fell while making his way through the snow. Eventually, he wore a path across the lawn to her grave.

"I still miss her," he said in 2009, dabbing his eyes with a handkerchief while standing beside her headstone. "I love my wife very much."

He said he thought of Katima all the time. "If I'm sitting alone, I'm always thinking of my wife."

Sometimes, while watching TV in his home, he would catch a whiff of Joy, the perfume she liked to wear. Sometimes he detected a hint of it in the cemetery too. One of the dog-walkers who frequented the burial park once told him he saw a woman standing behind Chan at the graveside.

Chan's daily journey continued until a couple of years before he died. A fall forced him into a care home. He had balked at making the transition before that, knowing it would mean the end of his visits. His relatives estimate that prior to his fall, Chan had only missed fifty-four days in more than sixteen years, and only when doing so was unavoidable—a medical procedure, a cancelled bus, something like that. Perfectly reasonable, to everyone but Chan. "It really upset him, because it was a promise," says his niece, Annia Lee.

He was also troubled by the attention his story received after I retold it in 2013, and he asked that I not drag it up again. "He was very private, quiet," Lee said. So, I didn't mention it again, not until learning from Chan's family that he had died at age eighty-six and that it was time for the final paragraph to a great romance.

"It was," says Lee, "a fairy tale."

Hipster Check

NEWS ITEM: Victoria is the highest-ranking Canadian
entry on a list of the most-hipster cities in the world.

SPUN TOWARD HER. "THE man bun isn't coming in as well as I
hoped. Where's my tuque?"

"The one that keeps your head warm, or the one you wear
like a baggie beanie with your ears showing?" she replied.

I almost choked on my avocado toast. "Beanie, of course.
What, you think I come from Vancouver?" I said "Vancouver"
as though I were trying to scrape it off the soles of my Chuck
Taylor All Stars.

Poor Vancouver finished well down the ranking of the
world's most-hipster cities: 199th place, sandwiched between
Braunschweig, Germany, and, I believe, Walmart. Quick, somebody call the grief counsellors.

Victoria? No. 1 in Canada, baby. Not that this is news to us.

Remember, it wasn't long ago that both *Vogue* magazine
and the *Toronto Star*—using the stunned tones of someone who
had just stumbled across Stephen Harper chained to a pipeline
while chanting "Keep the oil in the soil"—described Victoria
as this country's version of Portland, Oregon. They rattled on
about our locavore foodie scene, craft beer, and the gazillion
high-tech companies run by flannel-clad young people in funky
old brick buildings downtown. More recently, the *New York
Times* declared Victoria an "urban jewel." That was followed by
an enthusiastic travel piece in the *Wall Street Journal*, which
fell in love with what it called "funky Fernwood," bubbling on
about the drinkeries around the Belfry Theatre, the outdoor
book-exchange boxes, century-old Arts-and-Crafts bungalows,

community gardens, and Cold Comfort's "improbable but successful combination of vanilla ice cream and brown ale."

So, no, we're not surprised by our placing in the International Hipster Index.

Now, an embittered Vancouverite might point out that the index was compiled not by an institute of higher learning but by something called MoveHub, an international relocation-planning company whose commitment to rigorous scholarship might not be as unwavering as, say, Oxford's.

Nonetheless, MoveHub came up with its findings by comparing the number of vegan eateries, coffee shops, tattoo parlours, vintage boutiques, and record stores per 100,000 residents in 446 cities in 20 countries. Topping the list was the English seaside's Brighton and Hove, which just edged out Portland, Oregon. Salt Lake City was third and Seattle fourth.

The same embittered Vancouverite might point out that MoveHub wasn't actually being complimentary when it decided to ask "What's the most hipster city in the world?" The preamble to its findings said it posed the question because "our pretentious brethren deserve attention. It's all they really want."

Also, this same plaid-clad-but-mad Vancouverite might, somewhat churlishly, note that while Victoria is No. 1 in the Great White North, it only ranks 88th in the world index. Being the most hipster city in Canada is like being the shyest Kardashian or the most reasonable voice at Question Period. It's all relative.

"It may surprise some people to learn that Canada is not particularly hipster," MoveHub declared. "Too dignified, probably. The hipster capital of Canada proved to be Victoria . . . which was competitive on vegan eats and record stores, but let down by its shoddy tattoo studio game."

Shoddy tattoo studio game? Are they serious? Victoria goes through more ink than the aforementioned *New York Times*. Everybody from your favourite barista to your parish priest has a mistranslated Mandarin character ("'Upholstery'? It says 'upholstery'?") etched into their neck. We're pretty sure even W.A.C. Bennett had a Guns N' Roses tat on his lower back.

And what's this "too dignified" nonsense? Obviously MoveHub has never seen a couple of Canajun hockey moms chucking knuckles at their kids' peewee Christmas tournament, or observed the wild-eyed hit-to-pass Pat Bay 500 race for the last ferry off Vancouver Island, or watched Victorians lose their inhibitions/undergarments/stomach contents at the Canada Day Celebration/Fête du Régurgitation bacchanal by the Inner Harbour.

That's the problem with these out-of-town evaluations: Stereotypes. It's like those publications that still insist on seeing Victoria as a sleepy outpost of Olde England. Note that the *Globe and Mail* once described the capital as a place where the word "hip" is usually followed by "replacement."

Victoria is a lot of things: hipsterish, a bit of Britain, a government city, a tech centre, a military town, a retirement haven, a coastal dreamscape, a tourist mecca ... Pick a pigeonhole. We'll fill it.

Slug Fest

STEPPED ON A BANANA slug barefoot the other day—to clarify, it was I who was barefoot, though I suppose the slug was too—which made me think of Donovan Saul.

Saul is—or was—the Banana Slug King of Thetis Island.

A biological collector, someone who, under government licence, collects specimens for education and scientific research, Saul actually had a catalog of forty items for sale, not just slugs.

Most of what Saul collected was marine life plucked from the saltchuck as he plied the west side of the Strait of Georgia in his six-metre boat: jellyfish, whelks, hermit crabs, scale worms, anemones, and the sexily named warty sea squirt. Occasionally, he'd range over to the west coast of the Island for gooseneck barnacles or giant sand fleas the size of cigarette butts.

For some reason, though, it was the banana slugs that made Saul famous—that stuck to him, as it were. He'd search for them in low, damp, fern-covered areas, or on the side of the road after the grass was cut, or in the garbage dump after it rained.

Knowing of Saul's quest, his Thetis Island neighbours kept slug buckets. Kids would bring slugs to him. Saul would immerse them (the slugs, not the kids) in a concoction that would anesthetize and kill them. Each would be injected with a preservative before being shipped (by snail mail, of course) to US biological-supply companies, the ones that provided university science labs with everything from frogs to human cadavers.

The slugs weren't Saul's most lucrative product (he'd sell maybe a thousand a year, at 50 cents US apiece), but they were the gooiest, impregnating his clothes with a thick mucus that proved impossible to get out. That's what most of us think of when thinking of slugs: destructive creatures that spread slime wherever they go and sometimes get elected president. In Victoria, the City of Gardens, the poky predators fill even the most Dalai Lama-ish of residents with the kind of lip-curling fear and loathing that people in other cities reserve for thieves, telephone scammers, and street mimes. Some pour salt on them. Some cut them in half with scissors. Some lure them into containers half-filled with beer, which the slugs drink before climbing into their little slug cars and driving into one another.

They aren't even good to eat. Like the appendix, throw pillows, or Montreal traffic cops, slugs have no apparent purpose. The thing is, not appearing to have a purpose is not the same as not having a purpose. Researchers get quite excited about unlocking the secrets of slug slime, which could bring about treatments for cystic fibrosis, infertility, and ulcers. Sticky yet elastic, it could lead to a better medical glue. In the olden days, West Coast Indigenous Peoples spoke of slime's analgesic properties. A newspaper letter-to-the-editor writer swore it eased his psoriasis. There's even talk that the chemical messages that slugs leave in slime trails—telling other slugs what direction they're taking, even identifying their gender—could one day lead to the creation of fast, powerful, chemically based computers.

Saul won't be part of it, though. He has moved on from biological collecting. Diving into the depths, getting stung by jellyfish, sticking his hands with sea urchin spines that never come out, searching log booms for sea gooseberries—it's a young man's game.

He misses it, though. "It was hands-on biology," he says. His daily commute, which consisted of descending the stairs from his waterfront home to his boat on the water, sure beat the daily haul from, say, Surrey to Vancouver.

Saul still has no time for black arion slugs. They're an invasive species, just like American bullfrogs or your in-laws from Alberta.

He has a soft spot for our native green slugs, though. "If I see one, I try not to hurt it. If they're in the way, I pick them up and move them so they don't get hurt."

Beauty is in the eye, or perhaps the toes, of the beholder.

The Rogue Cow of Metchosin

AFTER TWO MONTHS ON the run, the Rogue Cow of Metchosin has been fenced in again, and I am sad.

No more will she emerge from her hideout in the hills to graze alongside her friends the deer. No longer will her sudden appearance on the forest's edge spook horses. No more will we be able to live vicariously through an animal that dared to dream of freedom.

This story goes back to one spring day in rural Metchosin, outside Victoria, when a previously placid cow suddenly lifted her head, gazed across a hedgerow, then leaped over it like an East German vaulting the Berlin Wall. No one knows why she bolted for freedom. Maybe she caught a glimpse of a grocery store flier, got a hint of what was to come. Or maybe she just had that gene that makes some folks peer over the hayfield horizon.

In any event, the Rogue turned into a bovine version of the Barefoot Bandit, a *Far Side* cartoon come to life. She spent the summer living wild, Huck Finning off the land, grazing in convenient fields, spearing catfish, shoplifting produce, shaking down children for their lunch money, and hotwiring unsecured farm vehicles.

Sometimes she would be spotted hanging out with the deer (for real) or taunting cattle and horses from the free side of a fence. One horse was spooked so badly that it broke out of its paddock and had to get its hips adjusted by an equine chiropractor. (Hands up, everyone who didn't know there was such a thing as an equine chiropractor.)

The Rogue had a bit of swashbuckling Robin Hood swagger to her, thumbing her nose at The Man by periodically popping up in public—startling Galloping Goose Trail hikers, or scaring the manure out of drivers when her ninja-black bulk would suddenly loom in the middle of a darkened road. Then she would slip into the woods before the Bossy posse would arrive. The farmer who owned the heifer chased her for kilometre upon kilometre to no avail, though he did discover where every black bear in Metchosin lived.

The thing is, the longer she remained at large, the larger her legend—and fan club—grew. This should not be a surprise. When human-owned animals break loose, people often root for the runner.

It happened with Lucy the Emu, the man-sized flightless bird that nonetheless took flight from a Nanaimo-area farm in 2014. They caught him (yes, Lucy was a he) eventually, but for six days the only thing captured was the public's imagination as the emu Thelma-and-Louised through the bush.

It happened with the two capybaras that became instant folk heroes after busting out of Toronto's High Park Zoo and running wild for several weeks in 2016. (Their three offspring were named after the members of the band Rush.)

And it happens a lot with cattle. Who can forget Yvonne, the dairy cow who became a German media darling after taking to the woods? She evaded capture for three months despite a 10,000 euro bounty, a shoot-to-kill order, and an attempt to woo her with what was described as "the George Clooney of bulls."

In another case, a Charolais cow who remained on the lam for eleven days after leaping a six-foot fence to escape an Ohio slaughterhouse was christened Cincinnati Freedom by artist Peter Max, who was allowed to take her into his care after offering US$180,000 worth of paintings to the SPCA. She lived out her days at an animal sanctuary in New York state.

In Massachusetts, a heifer named Emily managed to elude capture for forty days, some say with the help of sympathetic townsfolk. A full-size bronze statue of Emily now stands over her grave.

Conversely, no one built a monument or launched a save-the-slitherer campaign for the Snake In A Drain, a five-foot serpent discovered in a Victoria sewer pipe a couple of years back. (The corn snake did survive, though, going on to become a political analyst on Fox News.) Also, no one complained when the BC government announced open season on feral pigs, the descendants of farm escapees. To quote George Orwell: "All animals are equal but some animals are more equal than others."

Or maybe we just identify with some animals more than others. Maybe there's a little Rogue Cow of Metchosin in all of us, yearning to shed our shackles and clear the cubicle/corral.

In the end, after a summer chasing the Rogue around the wilds of Metchosin, the farmer finally found the key to reining her in: loneliness. The Hereford-Angus cross returned on her own, lured to the field from which she escaped by a small herd of cattle brought in specifically to entice her back. She just showed up at six o'clock one morning, no worse for wear. Not exactly fat, but not skinny, either, which seemed remarkable seeing how long she had been gone. After that the farmer took no chances, transferring the Rogue to a farm in Duncan, the equivalent of being shipped from a minimum-security prison to Shawshanksteak Penitentiary.

Knowing that she ended up back in cowstody might leaden the hearts of those readers who would have preferred that she had disappeared for good, joining the vanished-into-thin-air likes of D.B. Cowper or Jimmy Hoofa.

Those readers will be pleased, then, to learn the story had an unexpected epilogue. First, while I dubbed her the Rogue Cow of Metchosin, someone came up with a name more reflective of her elusive nature: Metchosin Moodini. Local artist Heather Buchanan used that name in designing a stylish poster, ensuring that the heifer's memory would live on long after the barbecue cooled.

Also, we learned that the Rogue/Moodini lives on in another way too: When she returned to that farmer's field, she was pregnant. Her calf is frolicking in a Metchosin field at this moment. No word on whether it was born half bovine, half bear, or whether it has horns or antlers.

Leaping Lizards

I **WAS OUT ON THE** deck tending the tomato plants, feeling vaguely Amish, when a tiny lizard sprang straight up in front of my face—boing!—as though shot from a jack-in-the-box. Somewhere, a little girl screamed. Wait, no, it was me. In my defence, the critter was creepy: Scaly skin, blank reptilian stare, tiny hands.

I poked my head inside the house: "Did you put LSD in the lemonade?"

"No."

"Then Vladimir Putin is in the garden."

She shook her head. "European wall lizard."

I grimaced. "No need to call me names."

"No," she said. "The European wall lizard is an invasive species that's spreading around southern Vancouver Island, just like grey squirrels, American bullfrogs, and Albertans. Conventional wisdom says they're descended from a dozen or so lizards that either escaped or were freed when Rudy's Pet Park, a private zoo on the Saanich Peninsula, closed in 1970."

"Right," I replied. "Where are the shotgun shells?" One minute you think you have a nice backyard, next thing you know it's Jurassic Park.

This is how we tend to react to lizards. With the exception of the GEICO gecko, they get a bad rap in popular culture. Spider-Man has an arch-villain named the Lizard. Sleazy guys are lounge lizards. When Edwin Edwards, the corrupt governor of Louisiana, ran against a former leader of the Ku Klux Klan, the bumper stickers read "Vote For The Lizard, Not The Wizard."

Victorians, who would, without a second thought, take a bullet for a UVic bunny, turn positively primal when encountering lizards, flailing at them with garden implements and flaming patio tiki torches. This is particularly true of wall lizards, which are frighteningly fast, the Connor McDavids of the reptile world.

Not that we are necessarily kind to the other wildlife that inhabit the city. Our ambivalence toward the urban deer that raze our flower beds, ignore traffic signals, and talk loudly on their phones in restaurants is well documented. Likewise, even Elizabeth May must stifle the urge to grab a shotgun and go Elmer Fudd on the thousands of once-transient, now-permanent geese that turn every local park, beach, and golf course into the world's grossest Slip 'N Slide. For the past three or four years, trained hawks have been used to shoo sidewalk-fouling, car-splatting gulls and pigeons away from downtown Victoria. (This is not the first time raptors have been used in this way. In the 1990s, after Victoria brought in falcons to scare starlings away from city hall, an unhappy *Times Colonist* letter-to-the-editor writer answered the question of where the startled starlings had been chased: "I'll tell you where they've falcon gone. They've gone to falcon Fairfield.")

As for cougars, the closer they get to downtown, the more alarmed we become. If they're spotted in farmin' country, it barely makes the news, the warnings sandwiched between stories about Joe Biden and whatever curiously innovative use of tax dollars Victoria council has came up with that day. Yet let one of the big cats run laps behind the legislature, as happened in 2015, and the cameras pursue it like it's O.J.'s white Ford Bronco.

One of the best cougar stories actually came from the Empress Hotel in 1992, when a big tom that wandered into the hotel's underground parking garage had to be tranquilized. Either that, or it fainted when it saw its parking bill. My colleague Mike Devlin, then a youthful Empress employee, got way too close to that cougar as it dashed past him in the parkade. Mike also had to be tranquilized.

Speaking of the Empress grounds, that's where Roger the yellow-bellied marmot (which sounds like something Yosemite

Sam would call Bugs Bunny) took up residence after hitching a ride on a transport truck. Politicians, conjuring up the spectre of an invasive species colonizing the Island, vowed to trap and deport Roger (or at least slap him with a foreign-buyers tax). It took at least four failed attempts to capture the marmot before someone thought to ask how, with no other yellow-bellies to mate with, he was supposed to breed and colonize. Basically, yellow-bellied marmots are like pipeline supporters: there might be a gazillion in Alberta and the BC Interior, but there was only one in downtown Victoria. After that realization, Roger (he was named after Empress manager Roger Soane) was not only spared but lavished with affection (and carrots).

We're being urged to show a similar lack of restraint with the European wall lizards. No reason to freak out, we're told. Wall lizards won't eat you or your pets (unless you have a pet cricket). There is no proof that they're harmful.

"OK," Island xenophobes reply, fondling the shotgun, "but neither is there proof that they aren't."

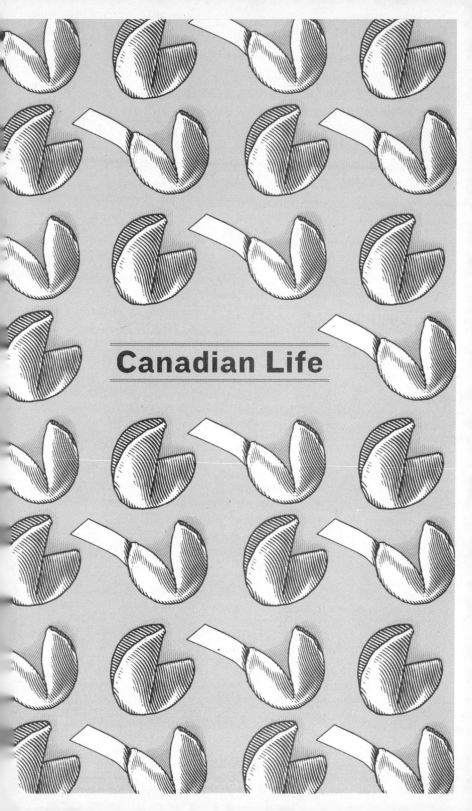

Canadian Life

The Thirteenth-Sexiest Accent

NEWS ITEM: A poll says Canadians have the thirteenth-sexiest accent in the world.

—*News.com*, Australia

SHE NUZZLED MY EAR. "Say, 'Roll up the rim to win.'"

I shook her off. "Charlize, baby, I told you it's over."

She kept going. "Now do the Friendly Giant: 'I'll call Rusty.'"

"I'll call the cops," I replied, peeling her hand off my knee. Really, it was like trying to get rid of cling wrap.

We've all been there, of course. One minute you're minding your own business in the Seattle airport, trying to convince the bartender that your old Canadian Tire money is legal tender, and next thing you know you're being pawed like it's feeding time at the SPCA.

Even a South African like Charlize—second-sexiest accent on the planet, by the way—couldn't resist the tundra-and-timber timbre of the typical Canuck.

This was confirmed by the release of that survey. Tourism site Big 7 Travel conducted the poll. They gave 8,500 people from 60 countries a list of 100 accents and asked them to rank their favourites. For the record, New Zealanders were deemed to have the sexiest voices, followed by Charlize's Afrikaans, the Irish, Italians, Aussies, and Scots.

The US Southern drawl was the top 'Merican accent, in ninth place. Canadian was sandwiched between twelfth-place standard English—the "clear, clipped, posh" Queen's English—and fourteenth-place Hungarian. Thirteenth out of a hundred. Not bad, eh?

But wait. What exactly did they mean by "Canadian accent?" It's not as though we have just one (or one language, for that matter).

I decided to try an experiment and gave her my best bilingual Montreal Canadiens rinkside announcer impression: "Mesdames et Messieurs, ladies and gentlemen, la première étoile, the first star, Guy Lafleur!" She appeared uncertain for a second, then pressed on. "Say 'tuque,'" she urged, throatily. "Two-four. T4 slip. Skookum. Block heater cord. Ian Hanomansing. Seven o'clock Eastern, 7:30 in Newfoundland."

Right, Newfoundland. There's another variation, b'y, and a charming one at that. When it comes to the cheerfully acerbic, pomposity-pricking smartarsery of Rick Mercer or Mary Walsh, it's a toss-up whether the accent accents the wit or the wit makes the accent that much more attractive.

Still, it wasn't clear whether that was what the Big 7 Travel survey had in mind. Probably they were thinking of Rachel McAdams or Ryan Reynolds or Ryan Gosling or one of our many, many other Ryans.

Or maybe the world is still going googly-eyed over Justin Trudeau—though his speaking voice is hardly his greatest asset. Our prime minister may be hotter than the August long weekend, but if there were a drinking game where you knocked back a Lucky every time he punctuated a sentence with "uh," we'd all be like Stalingrad: bombed around the clock.

Also, consider this: More than one-fifth of all Canadians were born outside Canada. That they don't all sound like Peter Mansbridge or Rosemary Barton doesn't make them any less Canadian.

Also, it's not as though all those who are native-born speak the same either. More than a century ago, visiting English poet Rupert Brooke wrote of being smitten with "the rather lovely sound of the soft Canadian accent in the streets." Apparently Brooke didn't walk down the same streets as Don Cherry.

And accents change over time. Some linguists say that we have, for the past quarter century, been going through what they call the Canadian Vowel Shift. Sounds are coming from higher and farther back in the mouth. "God" sounds like "gawd," "think" like "thenk."

That doesn't necessarily mean we sound more American. Our accents still differ, just in different ways than they did before. Canadian Mary Pickford was able to pass herself off as America's Sweetheart in the silent movies but ran into trouble when required to say her lines out loud: "The dialogue director had cautioned me so much about my Canadian 'r's' that I was terrified every time I said the word 'garden,'" she said. Today, it's words like "pasta" and "been," pronounced "pawsta" and "bin" in the US, that are coached out of Canadian actors.

"Or," I told Charlize, "perhaps I'm getting too worked up about an online poll that might not have been subjected to the kind of rigorous scrutiny as, say, a study published in the *New England Journal of Medicine*."

Her nostrils flared. "Now say 'double-double.'"

Good Morning, School

GOOD MORNING, STUDENTS. THIS will be the final set of announcements of the school year here at East Saanich High.

Please ensure your lockers are completely empty before leaving the school today. Mr. Arthurs the custodian wishes to pass on the following message: "If one of you little savages leaves another egg salad sandwich for me to find in August, I swear I will track you down, gut you like a wildebeest in the Serengeti, grind your entrails into the earth, and stake your head on the soccer field as a warning to the others." Also, Mr. Arthurs asks that all Scotch Tape be removed from locker doors.

Today's Grade 11 Principles of Math final exam has been cancelled due to an unfortunate accident involving the supervising teacher, Mr. Wilson, who was involved in a collision between a southbound car that left Nanaimo at 8:35 AM, travelling at an average of eighty-two kilometres per hour, and a northbound vehicle that left Victoria at the same time, travelling at a constant seventy-six kilometres per hour. In lieu of the exam, students are asked to answer the following question, as devised by the teachers' union: "Given that BC educators are paid far less than their counterparts in Ontario and Alberta, it would only be fair to award them a raise of A) 24 percent over three years, B) 24 percent over three years, or C) 24 percent over three years."

Students are reminded that even though it is the end of the school year and the warm weather has returned, the dress code remains in effect. Visible thong underwear, strapless tops, and shirts that expose the midriff are banned. Boys caught wearing such items will be forced to put on the puka shells, platform shoes, and Bay City Rollers tartan pants left here by their grand-fathers in 1976.

A tip of the hat to Chemistry 12 student Randall Ahiro for a really good try at the regional science fair, and our thanks to the paramedics and the hazardous materials response team for their prompt and courageous response.

Ms. Cheng notes that some Socials 10 students have yet to return their copies of the textbooks *What Next for the Soviet Union?* and *Here Come the 1970s*. Please return them in good condition, as they are not due to be replaced for at least another ten years.

Today's debate on classroom overcrowding has been can-celled on the order of the fire marshal.

Thanks to those who took part in the Re-Title the Teams con-test following the Human Rights Tribunal's declaration regarding our traditional names, the Fighting Indians and Squabbling White People (and White Peoplettes). The new name, as chosen by random draw, is the Perennial Losers, submitted by student I.M. Joe King. Mr. King, the football team's defensive front four would like to talk to you behind the gym after school.

The final meeting of the Attention Deficit Disorder Club will be held this afternoon at hey, is that a new shirt you're wearing?

Music fans should gather in the multi-purpose room at noon today, where East Saanich High's own hip-hop band Killa Thug Life will play their original composition Hungry Gangsta Ghetto Pain before their mothers arrive in the minivans to take them back to the mean streets of Broadmead.

Yearbooks are available for pickup in the library. Remember when signing them that they will be read by your future spouses and children in twenty years. Think of your yearbook comments as permanent literary tattoos.

Congratulations to Industrial Education teacher Mr. Carruthers on yet another successful reattachment surgery. Hope to see you in the fall, Lefty!

Congratulations are also due to those students who helped the lost and found department reach this year's goal of one thousand unclaimed Tupperware containers. Mrs. Johnson will staff the lost and found until 3:00 PM today. Please do not ask her if anyone has found your lost innocence or virginity. She has heard these side-splitting witticisms before.

Vice-Principal Tremblay wishes to salute the resourcefulness and ingenuity of this year's grad class. Now get his car off the roof before he calls the cops. Also, bring his wife back.

That is all. Enjoy your summer.

BC Daze

"**S**TART ME UP," SANG Mick.

"No," I replied. "If I start you up, you'll never stop."

Well, he couldn't deny that, so he shut up.

Mick is my belt sander. Do I often hold conversations with power tools? Of course not. Mostly they're down in the shop while I'm up on the couch with the channel changer, so we seldom get the chance to chat.

"We don't talk any more," Mick moaned when I hauled him out from behind the cracked extension cords and dried-up buckets of drywall paste.

"Talk?" I replied. "We don't even see each other."

I had dragged him out because I had to repaint the garage door, just as I have had to repaint the garage door for a few summers now. But painting means sanding, and who wants to waste a sunny day sanding? It's one of life's little ironies that certain jobs can only be done on days that are too nice to do them.

So Mick never did get plugged in. Back in the box, buddy. See you next year.

"Hey, Jack," called the air mattress as I stowed Mick away. "How about a dip in Matheson Lake?"

"Super idea," I replied.

"Me too!" called my fishing pole.

But then my wife called down the stairs: "Who are you talking to?"

"Um, Matt and Rod."

"Nice try," she said. "Go get Sandy."

"His name is Mick," I replied. "But he's sleeping. Besides, it's BC Day."

Well, she couldn't come back on that one. It would be flat-out sacrilege to force a fellow to pick up tools on the holiest day on the Lotus Land calendar. We do, after all, have a reputation to live up (or down) to. This is British Columbia, Canada's flaky, hedonistic, granola-smoking prodigal son. Mañana North. Canadians with ambition head for Toronto. Those who plan on being ambitious next week turn west until they get wet. Career-minded Easterners try to claw their way into a suit, tie, and premature heart attack. Out here, the goal is a job where you don't have to wear shoes. Or pants. At least, that's how the rest of the nation likes to think of us.

Work on BC Day? We'd be letting down the country. Would Ryan Reynolds let down the country? No, he wouldn't. Be like Reynolds, BC, don't let Canada down. Go to the lake. Or so I explained to my wife.

It reminds me of a long-ago summer when I was toiling in the paper mill at Ocean Falls, where it rains 452 days a year. During a rare dry spell, I picked up a bunch of double shifts because my replacement, a Newfoundlander, didn't show up for work.

"It was sunny, b'y," he later explained to the foreman, speaking slowly, as to a child. "I went fishin'." Why, he seemed to ask, would anyone voluntarily wander into the smelly belly of a mill when the Almighty obviously intended him to stay outside and catch salmon?

He was right. We live in Paradise on Earth: Towering mountains, inviting waters, blue skies right out of *The Simpsons*. German tourists spend fortunes to frolic here. Albertans dream of retiring on the green side of the Rockies. The travel magazines consistently rate us among the most desirable destinations on the planet. To ignore all this, to put our shoulders to the wheel when our heads should be in the clouds, would be to ignore God Himself. Which, again, I explained to my wife.

"Disappoint Ryan Reynolds if you want," I admonished her. "But I would think twice before disappointing God."

"Amen!" echoed the life jacket, hanging on the wall.

"Stay out of this, Bob," she warned him.

But there was no conviction in her voice. It was, after all, the BC Day long weekend. Next time it comes, around, go outside and play. The nice weather won't last forever. And if you're scheduled to work, call up and say, "Sorry, I feel well. I won't be in today."

Family Free Agency

NEWS ITEM: There's a free-agent frenzy as a record number of National Hockey League players are dropped by their old teams or choose to join new ones.

Hmm, makes you wonder what life would be like if families worked that way . . .

—Dean Cleveshaw, *The Canadian Press*

VICTORIA—TEAM KNOX ANNOUNCED SATURDAY it has inked veteran Jack Knox to a multi-year contract, ending weeks of speculation that he would be moving on.

"He has re-signed and we are resigned," muttered a subdued Mrs. Knox, the team's general manager, slumped behind a microphone at a hastily called press conference on the family's ill-tended back lawn. No other family members were present at the announcement, though a child could be heard weeping in the distance.

Knox, who can play both husband and father, has been with the organization for more than thirty years, though observers note he has lost much of his foot speed and most of his hair in recent seasons.

His best years came in the early 1990s, when he remembered every family birthday, didn't miss work, and successfully installed a ceiling fan without starting a house fire. However, his productivity soon tailed off, to the point that the team had to rush in raw, unproven teenage talent to program the home-entertainment system and reseat the toilet after he tried to drown the channel changer when the Canucks lost to Boston in 2011. The low point came when he burst his own appendix rather than spend Christmas with the in-laws. At work, he became such a non-entity that long-time colleagues began referring to him as "that new guy." His drop in effectiveness was reflected in his declining salary.

On Saturday, Knox defended his falling numbers. "My game has changed," he said. "I'm more of a stay-at-home, defensive-type husband these days. I like to think I can anchor the back end."

His wife replied that Knox was indeed stay-at-home— "couldn't get his lazy butt off the couch with dynamite and a forklift" is the way she put it—but added that he was "plenty offensive."

She agreed that he was an anchor.

The signing put to rest rumours that the team was prepared to cut Knox loose, that it had actively encouraged him to test the free-agent market. One child was known to drift away from him in supermarket checkout lines, pretending to be with other fathers, ones who didn't force their offspring to smuggle shop-lifted condiments past the cash register. ("Stop your whining," he was once heard to say. "They don't jail juveniles.")

What remains to be seen is how strained relations will be in the wake of a year-long lockout that began after Knox stepped out for a beer and accidentally spent the family college fund on a new Ford F-350 pickup truck. On the positive side, buying a truck that big gave him a place to sleep for the year. He also pointed out that his transgression wasn't as bad as that of the neighbour, who went out for a carton of cigarettes and came back with a case of venereal disease.

Knox told the press he looked forward to ending his playing days in the same sweater in which he began them. Ditto for the fortrel pants and leisure suit. "She keeps trying to donate them to the Salvation Army, but they keep giving them back," he said.

"Anyway, I think I got a few good years left and want to fin-ish my career here," the aging veteran added. "Not too many husbands get to spend their entire adult life with the same franchise."

At this point, the franchise collapsed on the lawn, her body wracked by great, heaving sobs, and the press conference ended.

In Praise of Ugly Trucks

ACCORDING TO CRIME STATS, pickup trucks are among the most commonly stolen vehicles on Vancouver Island. This brings three thoughts to mind:

A) When bad guys steal trucks, do their friends want them to help move house?

B) Given that the typical new truck now costs more (and is larger) than a home in small-town Saskatchewan, you can see why they're worth stealing.

C) Truck theft isn't a problem for me, since I haven't owned one for twenty years. I can't justify it, not with climate change leering through the window. Wanting a truck isn't the same as needing one, and I rarely have to transport anything more skookum than the occasional five-gallon drum of Miracle Whip or tire-sized wheel of cheese from Costco. (Never shop when you're hungry.)

Even when I did own trucks, they weren't worth swiping. Any pickup I piloted had passed its best-before date long before I got the registration papers. Odds are that any self-respecting thief would take one look, feel pity, and then slip a $20 bill behind the sun visor.

My favourite truck was one my wife dubbed the Babe Magnet, though I suspect this might have been sarcasm. Oh lordy, it was beautiful, a '79 Chevy, rust on blue on rust. Cracked windshield, no horn, shredded upholstery, a wire coat hanger where the aerial used to be, and a radio that would only play country music. It used to have two gas tanks, but one fell off. (My friend Les Leyne once poured gas all over his shoes because I forgot to tell him about that.) I got a speeding ticket on the Sookeihalla (as the highway west of Victoria is known) one night; when the Mountie asked why I was in such hurry, I just shrugged, because I didn't think it would help to explain that the dashboard lights didn't work and I had no idea how fast I was going.

The best part of the truck was the swan-in-flight hood ornament that would guide me home through the rain and fog. I liked to think it lent the truck an air of majesty. Indeed, my wife said if you squinted at the ornament just right, you might think you were riding in a Rolls Royce (though, again, this might have been sarcasm). Others also valued the swan: the most solid piece of the vehicle, it resisted many attempts by the jealous (or drunken) to wrest it from the hood.

Alas, the swan was grounded one day when, with the cordwood-laden Babe Magnet pointed into the bush, the transmission decided it no longer did reverse. I wanted to cut a path through the trees and keep driving forward, but I was dissuaded by my wood-cutting buddy. It was, literally and figuratively, the end of the road. I wept. My buddy wept. A single raindrop fell from the swan's eye. The Babe Magnet was no more.

That is, until a few years later when, having accumulated sufficient karma (truckma?), it was reincarnated as a little 1978 Datsun pickup that I bought for $500. It was another battered beauty: an even more badly cracked windshield, terminal backfires, dangerously rusted, painted a hideous yellow reminiscent of the Day-Glo toxic sludge that BC Ferries used to slop on its Sunshine Breakfast. (Remember the Sunshine Breakfast? If so, just place your head between your knees until the nausea fades.) Best of all, it had a pair of mysterious, large-calibre bullet holes that went in one side of the box but not out the other. The never-answered question: What stopped the slugs? Of course, I transferred the swan hood ornament to the Datsun, having wisely rescued it from the Chevy in anticipation of just such an opportunity.

About now, you might be asking yourself if there is a point to all this drivel. Well, no, other than a heartfelt desire to share with the world my love for ugly trucks.

I know I'm not alone in this sentiment. I had a co-worker who used to kick a new dent in the Chevy now and then, just to add to its beauty.

There was also the day that an acquaintance of one of the many former owners of the Datsun pulled up next to me at a traffic light and excitedly yelled, "I had sex with half of the women in Victoria in the back of that truck!" I didn't know how to reply to that, so lamely stammered something about just using it to haul bark mulch.

I question the motives of this last fellow but have no doubt about the touching sincerity of others who have greeted my trucks the way they would welcome a beloved, if somewhat disreputable, cousin.

What is it about a beat-up pickup that elicits in some the kind of adoration that Trudeau can only dream of? Dunno. Perhaps it's the same plucky underdog thing that attracts us to mongrel mutts, Jamaican bobsledders, or whatever independent bookstores the online giants are Darth Vadering on any given day.

Or maybe we view it as an automotive version of what we hope others see in ourselves: nothing much to look at, but dependable when needed and, damn, but you'd miss it if it were gone.

Our Bulging Wastelines

"**G**REAT," I THOUGHT WHEN we moved into the new house. "It doesn't need any work at all."

"We'll start with the bathroom," she said.

Oh well, at least I got to take the renovation rubble to the garbage dump.

This may not seem like a big deal to those who find their spiritual renewal in, say, church. But for men of a certain disposition, there is nothing so cleansing, so reinvigorating, as a pilgrimage to the local landfill. Women go to the spa. Guys go to the dump. There's something refreshing about standing in the box of a truck, shucking junk like bad memories and worse habits, getting rid of life's clutter. Not long ago, BC's Sons of Freedom Doukhobors would shed their clothes and burn their own homes to show contempt for materialism. Really, all they had to do was drive to the landfill instead. This is particularly true in spring, when the world is knee-deep in new beginnings. The blossoms are opening, and so are opportunities for change.

Time to get rid of the old and the useless, she said, or at least send him off to do some chores. So I borrowed a friend's truck and carted away all sorts of junk I no longer need: old linoleum, a tire swing, a rusted burn barrel, Conrad Black's autobiography . . .

Even driving the truck was a treat. I miss my old pickup—not the one with the unexplained bullet holes in the box, but the half-ton with the coat-hanger aerial that brought in nothing but AM country and western stations. ("Life in the saddle just ain't been the same since my horse died," I wailed. "I can't get over you, so why don't you get under me." It's even better with a dog to sing the harmony.)

Alas, I had to have that pickup put down. I replaced it with a series of more sensible, grown-up vehicles, until one morning I suddenly found myself driving to work in a four-door Volvo, listening to classical music and wearing a Harris tweed jacket. I would have veered off the bridge right then and there were it not for the damned guardrails.

But I digress. We're supposed to be talking about trash, not trucks.

At the dump, the first thing you do is weigh in, pulling up on the scales and talking into a speakerphone like they use at the McDonald's drive-through. Next time you're at the landfill, order a cheeseburger and fries. I bet they never get tired of that line, or of overcharging you after you use it.

They never used to have scales. In the old days, you could wheel right into the dump, pull up to the shore of the Great Garbage Sea, and start hucking junk off the back. There were always a few guys hanging around, ready to scoop up the good stuff. It was literally a free-for-all, recycling before its time. Once, I tossed out a creased metal garbage can lid, only to see an eighty-year-old man dart out and snatch it on the first bounce like a shortstop fielding a hot grounder. That old guy could really move.

Things are much more orderly today. Now there are Rules, with a capital R: Wood waste over here, metal over there, special handling for the bits that might blow up spectacularly were you to plug them with a .22. (I can still hear my mother's voice: "What are you kids doing inside on a nice day like this? Get your guns and go to the dump.") Rules may be good for the environment, but they're bad for the soul. The dawn of Rules at the garbage dump was like the arrival of barbed wire in the Old West—the end of the great, untamed frontier. Now the pastures are fenced in, the buffalo are gone, and orange-vested, hard-hatted marshals ride the rubbish range, enforcing the law.

Some dumps even refuse refuse: no dog droppings, no paint cans, no drywall. No car batteries or auto parts of any description—a low-carburetor diet for governments worried about their growing wastelines. Big cities can't find anywhere to take their trash. Garbage, like downtown drug dealers getting shuffled from corner to corner, doesn't so much disappear as merely go somewhere else. And somewhere else doesn't want it.

Toronto, for example, once sent much of its waste—one million tonnes a year—to Michigan, but that state then passed a law to keep out the nastiest trash. Which means no more road trips for the Maple Leafs.

There was a plan to ship Toronto's rubbish six hundred kilometres to an abandoned mine in northern Ontario, but Kirkland Lake residents rejected the idea. This confounded Torontonians, who couldn't fathom anyone rejecting World Class Trash from what they keep assuring us is a World Class City ("I'm pretty, aren't I? AREN'T I?").

Actually, Canadians in general have a reputation for sending waste abroad. Remember that fuss in 2019 when the president of the Philippines threatened war if we didn't take back 103 shipping containers of what were supposed to be recyclables but turned out to be household trash? At the time, we were told that Canadians produce more solid waste per capita than any other people on Earth. That's embarrassing. So is the idea of using other countries as our garbage dump.

Canada should buy a pickup truck. And a dog. And it should get rid of its own garbage in its own back yard.

David Graham

F YOU'RE LIKE ME, you have more negative role models than positive ones.

You see somebody berating a restaurant server, or going off his nut in traffic, or getting in a Twitter war, or puffing up with self-righteous indignation, and you tell yourself, "Don't be that guy."

But then there was David Graham.

I met him after he drove out from Ontario in 2001, a rowing shell lashed to the roof of his car (he had come achingly close to qualifying for the 1984 Olympics), to become principal of Metchosin's West-Mont School.

Red-haired, bursting with energy, close to forty but looking closer to fourteen, he greeted each day like it was the front gate to Disneyland. His smile didn't appear to have an off switch. Neither did he. My first thought was "Is he for real?" Yes, he was. All the time.

He eschewed the break-their-spirits school of schooling and was instead unrelentingly supportive of his students, building them up with a barrage of superlatives—"amazing," "fantastic," "awesome"—that would make cynics (OK, me) roll their eyes were he not both genuine and the living embodiment of the values he espoused. It also helped that he had a cheerfully mischievous sense of humour.

One of his old buddies would later offer a sample of the latter, recalling a long-ago summer-camp dance where the boys were introduced to the girls from the camp next door. The friend turned to a coughing David and said, "What's the matter, Red, got a frog in your throat?" "Yeph," David replied, allowing the frog, a live one held in his mouth, to leap out. Don't know how that worked with the girls at the dance, but he ended up with a gem in Jill, whom he met at the Queen's University rowing club. One of their first dates was to a zoo. She was smitten. "Here was a guy who didn't have to go to the pub to have fun," she would later tell the *Times Colonist*. "He invented fun."

Jill flew out with their three boys shortly after David arrived in Metchosin. They all moved into Victoria a few years later, when David became head of Glenlyon Norfolk's middle school. Wherever it was, the Graham house always felt a bit like a riot without the tear gas. It was non-stop joyful pandemonium, a confusion of kids, dogs, ball-hockey nets, and canoes, somebody always late for something, the consequence of trying to stuff ten pounds of life into a five-pound bag. "Let's go exploring," read the final panel of David's favourite *Calvin and Hobbes* cartoon and, sure enough, opportunities for new adventures rarely went unseized. One Friday in 2007, he decided to run the Royal Victoria Marathon two days later. He finished in under four hours, despite ducking into a coffee shop to say, um, I'm running out of gas, could somebody buy me a coffee and a muffin?

The next summer he suffered a seizure, the first sign of the brain cancer that took his life in 2009 at age forty-seven.

No point in going on about the unfairness of it all. No surprise that David's positive nature never failed him, even as his body did. No surprise that so many felt his loss so deeply; there were two memorial services, one in Ontario and one attended by close to a thousand people in Victoria. At the latter, Simon Bruce-Lockhart, then head of Glenlyon Norfolk School, summed David up perfectly: We are all modest some of the time, positive some of the time, happy, energetic, guileless, and selfless some of the time, he said, but David was those things all of the time.

"David was an extraordinary man because his virtues went clear through him—they were him day in and day out. What is episodic in us is just who he was ... You couldn't be in David's company without being reminded of your better self, and you couldn't leave his company without having been inspired to call upon that better self a little more often."

In 2021, Bruce-Lockhart was called on to speak again, this time at the dedication of the newly named and refurbished David Graham Learning Commons at the school. Imagine that, having an influence so strong that they name a library after you twelve years after you're gone. Bruce-Lockhart reminded the gathering that by the end, a stroke had robbed David of his ability to speak. Still, he could manage five phrases: "Thank you." "We're so lucky." "I love you." "Yummy." "Wow." It's the last one that still stuck with Bruce-Lockhart now. "'Wow' is about a sense for wonder and awe that we too often let rust beneath the tyranny of the immediate," he said. "'Wow' is the gift of being appreciative of the richness of potential around us."

That was David. His Olympic dream, his life, might not have had the ending anyone wanted, but the journey was amazing.

It's funny who we remember, what we remember about them, and for how long. Someone at the library dedication quoted David's sister as saying some people have a light so bright that it keeps shining even when they're no longer here.

David and Jill's sons, Patrick, Cameron, and Chris, all spoke. Chris remembered his dad telling him that over time, people will forget a lot of the details about you—the goals you scored, your accomplishments—"But they will never forget the way you treated them."

It's something to think about: Who we choose as our measuring sticks, what kind of people we aspire to be, and what it is about us that we hope people will remember, once all the stuff that doesn't really matter is gone.

Silos

"**N**OTHING YOU HAVEN'T SEEN on the beach," says the woman peeling down to her yellow underwear.

Sure, I think, staring at my shoes. A beach in the south of France.

We are upstairs in the Smoking Lily studio, a space not much larger than your rumpus room. It is packed with women pulling clothes on, pulling them off, adding garments to the purchase pile, or pitching them back like undersized salmon.

For the uninitiated, Smoking Lily is a trendy women's clothing shop in Victoria. Every year, shoppers line up for hours to get into its annual garage sale. Once inside, they attack their task with a businesslike efficiency that would make a German engineer weak at the knees, their approach less frantic than focused.

Women arrive dressed in ways that allow them to try on clothes without disrobing: slip-on shoes, tank tops, leggings under skirts. Other fashionistas somewhat discreetly strip to their skivvies without a second glance at the only guy in the room. I look like somebody's dad. Or maybe a creepy uncle.

I had heard about the annual Smoking Lily sale for years but thought it an urban legend, like the secret tunnels under Chinatown or a respectful and functional legislature. It's an insider's event, the time and place spread by word of mouth in the manner of a Dirty '30s bare-knuckle boxing match or a high school house party.

By the time the sale began at 1:00 PM, the line-up stretched around the block, pretty much everyone in the queue a young, attractive woman—not that I noticed, dear. One of those in line, a veteran of three previous sales, bore the expression of a prize-fighter gearing up for a championship bout. The woman with her, a newbie named Denise, just looked nervous: "I'm a little bit afraid."

Join the club, Denise. I've been less frightened at a gun-fight. I kept thinking of those 1940s stories of sales clerks being crushed in the frenzy when the Hudson's Bay store got its first shipment of post-war stockings, silk no longer being needed for Air Force parachutes.

We didn't even talk the same language, these Smoking Lily women and I.

"Connor McJesus," I said to one. "Lawnmower repair. Pickup truck. Mark's Work Wearhouse." But she didn't speak Middle-Aged Suburban Man.

"Fluevogs," she replied. "Appletinis. Hot yoga. Quinoa salad." I only caught every fourth word; my Hip Young Urban Woman is pretty rusty.

Lord knows what I was doing there. Fashion does not play as great a role in my life, as you might suspect. I have not chosen my own attire since the Trudeau Classic era. "Am I dressing like this for work? Of course not. These are merely my car-warming clothes. Remind me again of what it is I want to wear." (Speaking of Pierre, his face was silkscreened onto underpants sold at Smoking Lily; students of twentieth-century Canadian political history will appreciate the ironic comparison between the trendy Trudeau gaunch and their own dull, grey Stanfields, the latter getting their name from the same underwear-making family that produced lugubrious Progressive Conservative leader Robert Stanfield, whom Pierre beat in three straight elections.)

I was a fish out of water at the Smoking Lily sale, and that's the point. It does us good every now and then to wander into someone else's world. Ever notice that you run into some people all the time while seeing others so seldom that they might as well live on the Moon? Stay in the same orbit, keep to the same pattern day after day, and you'll never make a lunar landing, never see anything new. It has become worse in an age when we get all our news from silos of our own choosing, echo chambers in which our own voices bounce back at us with no room for unconsidered opinion or unexpected perspective. That's how the US ended up with a blue-red divide in which the two extremes are like an old married couple who have forgotten what they ever had in common. It's how Canadians end up yelling at, not talking to, one another.

I've always thought it would help bring us together if we could be dropped into each other's realities for a bit, just like those government-funded student exchanges that used to send young people from diverse backgrounds to unfamiliar parts of Canada with the goal of broadening horizons while not getting pregnant. We need an all-ages program like that, one where fifteen-year-old Montreal mall rats drive cattle in the Chilcotin, British Properties moneybags sling poutine in a Trois-Rivières casse-croûte, and Oshawa automakers swap places with immigrant care aides in a Calgary nursing home. Take Saskatchewan farmers to a potlatch on Vancouver Island and bus Halifax hipsters to the Williams Lake Stampede. Let Toronto bicycle couriers throw a curling stone at an outdoor bonspiel on Atlin Lake while a wolf howls at a 3:00 AM moon. Drag the carnivores from the Keg and have them sing "Give Peas a Chance" at a vegetarian restaurant.

Explore new worlds without leaving home. It would do us all good to walk a mile in another's shoes, whether they be gumboots or Manolos.

Oh, Canada

THEY CHANGED THE WORDS to the national anthem a few years ago, and I am still supposed to be outraged. Or proud. I can't remember which.

Proponents say replacing "in all thy sons command" with "in all of us command" advanced gender equality, but grumpy opponents saw it as either A) heritage being sacrificed for tokenism or B) the first step toward godless socialism, compulsory veganism, and the cancellation of *Coronation Street*.

Me, I plan to keep singing "O Canada" in the traditional manner: soundlessly.

This is what most people do. They either stand through the anthem blank-faced, as though waiting for a bus, or work their mouths like a trout gasping for breath at the bottom of the boat.

Some of us learned this in school, where we began each day by not joining the teacher in singing "O Canada" and ended it by not singing "God Save the Queen." Then the Trudeau 1.0 era arrived and we stopped not singing "The Queen" in favour of not singing "O Canada" in both official languages. That year, 1968, also marked the previous time we changed the lyrics to "O Canada," dropping two of the five (yup, five) "stand on guards," shuffling a couple of "O Canadas" and adding "from far and wide" and "God keep our land." That's when we really went into silent mode, since remembering the new words proved too taxing for people long used to singing the first four lines, then simply moaning "stand on guard, stand on guard" until the piano stopped.

Not that changing the words was anything new. There were, in fact, forty English-language versions of "O Canada" before Robert Stanley Weir's 1908 lyrics were adopted. And even that version was altered, with Weir's "thou dost in us command" giving way to "in all thy sons command" in 1913. The original French lyrics have remained unaltered since Judge Adolphe-Basile Routhier wrote them in 1880: "O Canada, terre de nos aïeux, Ton front est ceint de fleurons glorieux! Car ton bras sait porter l'épée, Il sait porter la croix!" (Translation: "O Canada! Land of our forefathers; Thy brow is wreathed with a glorious garland of flowers. Canadiens penalty to No. 14, Nick Suzuki, two minutes for tripping.")

That last bit might come as a surprise to English Canadians, who are generally less familiar with the French words to their own anthem than they are with those of the "Star Spangled Banner." Note that in 2014, after the singer's microphone died halfway through the American anthem, the crowd at a Toronto Maple Leafs game delivered a stirring a cappella rendition complete with the bit about being happy that "our" flag was still there, having survived the bombs bursting in air during the War of 1812—the one where we torched the White House.

That's about the only place you actually hear anthems anymore: at a game. This leads to an obvious question: Why? Why there and not, say, at the theatre or before staff meetings or ferry sailings? And when we are at a game, why do Canadians and Americans have to sing (or at least stand for) each other's anthems?

We do it because, well, it's habit. The National Hockey League decided in 1987 that both anthems must be sung whenever Canadian- and US-based teams meet, cementing a practice that had been common since the 1960s. Major league baseball and basketball follow the same rule (though it's applied relatively rarely, each sport having only one Canadian team). Again: Why? No disrespect to our well-armed neighbours, but "The Star Spangled Banner" means nothing to us. Might as well sing "Uptown Funk" or "Which Way You Goin' Billy?" American fans must feel the same way about "O Canada." Standing for somebody else's anthem is like listening to an aging relative describe his colonoscopy. It's something to be politely endured, not enjoyed. For one side, an anthem is an expression of national pride; for the other, it's the last pee break before the puck drops.

But I digress. We're supposed to be talking about lyrics here, not location.

It does seem odd that anglophones should get so worked up about a minor tweak to the English words to "O Canada" while not seeing anything odd about having a parallel, totally unrelated set of French lyrics to their own anthem. It's as though half of the US sang "O, say can you see" while the other half belted out the words to "Sweet Child o' Mine."

And if the "thy sons command" part was contentious, then how about that "Car ton bras sait porter l'épée, il sait porter la croix" line? It actually translates to "because your arm knows how to carry the sword, it knows how to carry the cross." That line should have atheist revisionists wetting their pants.

However, both the French and English lyrics are pretty benign when compared to the anthems of other countries. France's "La Marseillaise," for example, warns of foreign invaders "coming into our midst/To cut the throats of your sons and consorts." It goes on to urge the French to slaughter the foreigners: "Let impure blood/Water our furrows." Must make immigrants feel super welcome.

Mexicans sing "War, war! Let the national banners be soaked in waves of blood," Italians warble "We are ready to die," and Vietnamese trill "The path to glory is built by the bodies of our foes." Hungary's lyrics could have been penned by Kurt Cobain: "No freedom's flowers return, from the spilt blood of the dead, and the tears of slavery burn, which the eyes of orphans shed." By comparison, "O Canada" sounds as though it were written by Sharon, Lois, and Bram.

As for changing the words, how can you complain if you don't actually sing them?

The Census We Want

I **FILLED OUT MY CENSUS** questionnaire this week. Some households got the long form, but mine got the short one, which was a bit like opening *War and Peace* and discovering it's the *Reader's Digest* condensed version.

My census didn't ask me much at all: age, marital status, what languages I speak. I wanted to answer the language question with a knee-slapper of a story about getting confused and ordering half a railway with potato salad in a restaurant in Germany, or the time when I was seventeen and got decked in a broomball game in Quebec because I didn't know the French for "wanna fight?" ("Pardonnez-moi?" I replied brightly in my best BC junior secondary school French. It went downhill from there.)

Alas, the census people didn't allow for such answers, just brusquely moved me along to the next question, which had to do with my gender at birth and how I identify now. That's new, but not necessarily on my list of Top 10 Things You Want to Know About Your Fellow Canadians.

That's the thing about the once-every-five-years census. It does a nice job of measuring how Canada changes over time in terms of age, family makeup, religion, ethnicity, and so on, but it isn't great at answering the questions that spring to mind at beer o'clock.

To really gain our attention, the questions should go something like this:

1. Are you willing to fill out this census form?
    _ Yes.

_ No, Statistics Canada is just a front for the CIA/ United Nations/New World Order/Big Pharma and its lust for global domination and lower highway speed limits.

If you answered "yes," proceed to question 3. If "no," please answer question 2.

2. Your firearms are:
   _ Semi-automatic.
   _ Automatic.
   _ In the bunker, behind the Trump poster.

3. Sex:
   _ Male.
   _ Female.
   _ Nobody's business.
   _ Not tonight, dear, I have a census.

4. Age:
   _ Thong underwear.
   _ Bifocals.
   _ Seven-day pill organizer.
   _ Eat dessert first, just in case.

5. What's the worst lie you have ever told?

6. What is your greatest regret?

7. Do you believe in life after death?

8. How dopey will you feel (or not) if it turns out you're wrong about number 7?

9. Are you happy? If yes, jump to question 11. If no, proceed to question 10.

10. When people ask how you're doing, do you answer A) "Fine, thanks" or B) "Truly we lead quiet lives of desperation. How about them Canucks?"

11. How much did you drink during the first year of COVID?

12. Your mother's not here: How much did you really drink?

13. We promise that your answers are confidential. Have you ever cheated on:
    _ Your taxes?
    _ Your spouse?
    _ Your diet?
    If you replied yes to "taxes," proceed to question 14. If yes to "spouse," go to 15. If yes to "diet," at least you're honest. If no to any of the above, jump to 16.
14. We were lying about the confidentiality. Give us $50 or we're telling.
15. Ditto. Make it $5,000.
16. Starbucks or Tim Hortons?
17. Don Cherry or Kevin Bieksa?
18. Innie or outie?
19. Idris Elba or Bradley Cooper? Ginger or Mary Ann?
20. If you understood the Ginger or Mary Ann reference, jump to question 27.
21. Do you know what "cheugy" means? If so, jump to question 24.
22. Did you or anyone in your cohort ever have a haircut like Rachel from *Friends*? If yes, jump to question 26. If your answer is "Rachel, who?" jump to question 28.
23. Where do you stand on man buns? If you think they're not cheugy, jump to question 25. If your answer is "at the base, with both feet" go to question 29.
24. You belong to Generation Z, which means you say "OK Boomer" to Millennials. Question: Do you ever expect to move out of your parents' home?
25. You are a Millennial. Your chances of home ownership depend on: A) frugality, B) a strong work ethic, or C) your parents being hit by a bus.
26. You belong to Generation X, which means every dollar you earn goes to housing so you have been reduced to eating carpet underlay and selling spare children but that's OK because you're still living the dream, right? Right?

27. You are a Baby Boomer. What are your children most likely to inherit from you: A) the family home, B) a large collection of fanny packs, or C) a raging sense of entitlement?
28. Do you know where your seven-day pill organizer is?
29. What would you like for that dessert: A) apple pie or B) you can't find your teeth, better make it Jell-O.
30. On a scale of 1 to 10, how hot are you? If 10, how long have you written for the Times Colonist?
31. What is your greatest fear: A) climate change, B) COVID-19, C) the loss of a loved one, or D) bike lanes?
32. If D, how long have you lived in Victoria?
33. Do you use the census to see what sets us apart from one another, or to find what we have in common?

Dave and Morley

IS IT WRONG THAT I miss Dave and Morley more than I do Stuart McLean? I never met McLean, the much-loved CBC Radio storyteller who died in 2017, way too young at age sixty-eight. But Dave and Morley, the fictitious characters McLean created for *The Vinyl Cafe*, these were people we knew. They were good friends of twenty years. And now I miss them, perhaps not as much as I miss my old dog Spot, but more than I do some blood relatives.

We spent a lot of time together—weekends, sometimes, but more commonly on long road trips that would fly by once we got lost in the stories, many of which involved Dave trying to dig his way out of a hole and only making things worse.

It was hard to drive straight. You'd be cringing and laughing at the same time, tears falling on the steering wheel as Dave unravelled some tale of domestic disaster—the do-it-yourself electrical job that almost destroyed the kitchen, or the time he accidentally went for a ride on a bicycle locked to a car's roof rack, or Polly Anderson's Christmas party where the punch bowls got mixed up and the teenage daughter who tried to get drunk stayed sober but the pre-teen son ended up slurring "Come and get me, copper" at a traffic stop.

The Vinyl Cafe was like a marriage of Norman Rockwell and *The Simpsons*. Dave was a somewhat shambolic man, well meaning but forever tripping over his own flaws. First time I met him, he had swallowed a fly and, being a hypochondriac with an overactive imagination, was trying to extract it by placing his mouth over the bulb of a table lamp, drawing it to the light. Morley was pretty awesome too, but to me, Dave was like looking in a mirror. And now they're gone. Or, to be real, McLean is gone—and the nation is poorer for it.

"He was a Canadian ganglion, our connective tissue," his friend and colleague Shelagh Rogers wrote on CBC.ca. "He was our ear, our stethoscope."

Rogers wrote of the "thousands of people who came to *The Vinyl Café* in the grand necklace of theatres that dot our land, Stuart telling them stories about their community as though he'd been living there forever." He was good at creating characters who seemed familiar no matter where you lived.

Several years ago we took my mother to see McLean during one of his cross-Canada Christmas tours. It was everything you could hope for: relaxed and witty and warm (OK, stifling, we were high up at the back), the packed house eager for the retelling of stories they could recite by heart. When McLean began "Dave Cooks the Turkey" the crowd erupted in applause, just as it would had he been Paul McCartney playing the opening bars of "Hey Jude." It was great.

Except when we walked back to the car after the show, there was a homeless guy sleeping in a doorway. It was hard to ignore the contrast between the good-humoured, well-fed world inside the theatre and the reality on the street.

That's what a lot of humour does: reminds us that all is not well. From Stephen Leacock to the *Saturday Night Live* creator Lorne Michaels, Canada has produced a long line of satirists who mine the gap between life as it is presented and how it really is. The people who do that best often come from the edges of the country, which offers a different perspective on the absurdity of things. Rick Mercer is from Newfoundland, as are the cast members of *This Hour Has 22 Minutes*. Victoria's Ian Ferguson and his brother Will grew up in the far north of Alberta. Leacock Medal winner Susan Juby was raised in Smithers and lives in Nanaimo, on the edge of Canada. Adrian Raeside came from New Zealand. They're all good at calling bull.

But as much as satire is a means of pointing out that all is not as rosy as we are led to believe, it can also have the opposite effect, letting us know that things aren't that bad. McLean's humour was gentle and familiar and grounding, a reminder that there's more to the world than the anger and anguish that pours out of our screens all day. It's not all terrorism and tension. McLean—a three-time winner of the Leacock—took us to a fictitious community based in a common reality. It was a place where Dave and Morley dreamed and failed, felt joy and sorrow, and frequently endured the kind of heartache reserved for those who take on others' pain. If they occasionally crashed through the thin ice of human frailty, they were also good to the core.

Hurry Hard

"**H**URRY!" HE YELLED, WHITE knuckles gripping his broom. "HURREE HARRRRRRD!"

Jeez, buddy, I'm drinking as fast as I can. Can't a guy finish his beer? Apparently not. It's time for our game, so I get hustled out of the curling club lounge and down to the ice.

It seems curling is serious business, though what else would you expect from a sport played by Canadians, Scots, Swedes, and the Swiss? Not knee-slapping hilarity and volcanic passion, that's for sure. Or, as it said on the website when the World Curling Championships came to Victoria: "Come for the curling, stay for the excitement." I'm not making this up.

As true fans will tell you, curling is a game of precision and strategy, a marriage of the cerebral and the physical, requiring the mind of a chess master, the hand of a surgeon, and, traditionally, at least three fingers of rye.

It also demands a degree in linguistics, its arcane lexicon being as impenetrable as Chaucer. Here, for example, is how sportswriter Cam Cole's once wrote about a men's Olympic gold medal game: "It didn't hurt that the Canadians had Mark Nichols throwing third stones, either, because he shot the lights out, 97 per cent in the final, setting up the six-ender with a perfect raise double takeout that didn't even tickle the Canadian rock on the button, and a chip and roll behind cover after the Finnish skip twice wrecked on guards." A line like that should be on the citizenship test.

My own curling experience is limited to a single mixed-league season in the 1990s and then, some twenty years later, the event I referred to at the top: the City of Langford Mayor's Invitational Mid-Winter Blues Funspiel. Our cobbled-together newspaper team actually had highish expectations going into the funspiel, as our foursome included Darron Kloster, who is a farm boy from Luseland, Saskatchewan. Alas, it turned out that, as a curler, Darron is one of the best business editors Luseland ever produced.

"What do you mean you don't curl?" we asked, shocked, when he admitted as much five minutes before the first game. "You're from Saskatchewan. You have to curl. It's a law."

Damn. So much for our ringer. It reminded me of coach Harry Neale's line about Canucks defenceman Lars Lindgren: "Eight million Swedes and we get the only one who can't skate."

Anyway, the funspiel went downhill from there. I managed to lose every game and the crotch of my best pair of jeans. This, by journalism standards, qualified me as an expert, which is why I was happy to offer the following glossary of terms when the championship tournament came to town:

- **World Curling Championship:** Men's competition descended from the Scotch Cup, which was sponsored by the Scotch Whisky Association. The Canadian men's championship, the Brier, was sponsored by Macdonald Tobacco until 1980, followed by Labatt for more than twenty years, and then Tim Hortons. Scotch, cigarettes, beer, and doughnuts. Is this a great sport, or what?
- **house:** Circular target at either end of ice. Think of the old shuffleboard table in the bar, though curling no longer has ashtrays on the playing surface.
- **clean house:** What you do with your broom. Or the result of a "take-out" game.
- **take-out:** Yummy. A godsend during the pandemic.
- **ends and guards:** Football linemen. Have nothing to do with curling.
- **rock:** A smooth stone also known as a Scottish bocce ball. Made from rare, dense polished granite

quarried on the island of Ailsa Craig. Each weighs forty-two pounds, which equals C$96.

- **shot:** Traditionally single-malt Scotch, though some Canadian curlers prefer rye.
- **shot rock:** An ice cube.
- **the button:** Flies off the pants when crouching in the hack.
- **hack:** Any curling writer.
- **hog line:** Queue of hacks at press box buffet.
- **hack weight:** Usually about eight pounds heavier after the buffet.
- **the Hammer:** Nickname of former Philadelphia Flyer bad boy Dave Schultz. Curling doesn't have bad boys, bench-clearing brawls, steroid-shooting home-run hitters, or seven-foot multi-millionaires who talk about themselves in the third person. No doping scandals, either, unless Vicks VapoRub counts. Curlers are less likely to be hip than to break one and are unassuming to the point of invisibility. Curlers make Ron MacLean look like Justin Bieber by comparison. (This is not a bad thing.) Curling is a blend of bad fashion sense and good manners, not greed and testosterone. This is why it is broadcast at 9:00 AM on CBC, not prime time on Fox.
- **slider:** Awesome album recorded by T. Rex in 1972. Has nothing to do with curling, though there is a track titled "Rock On."
- **scoring:** Curlers score by buying "shots" for members of the opposite sex in the lounge, encouraging them to drop their "guard" and go to the "house." A successful "take-out" attempt is known as a "hit and roll."
- **sheet:** What curlers mutter after missing their shot or splitting their best pair of jeans.

Under the Influence

NEWS ITEM: In a bid to increase the youth vote, Elections Canada will spend $650,000 to enlist the help of thirteen "influencers," including social media stars, YouTubers, Olympians and a gamer.

—*Globe and Mail*

I **TURNED DOWN THE MUSIC** (K-Tel's *20 Power Hits*) so that she could hear what I had to say. "I'm going to be a youth social media influencer."

She paused. "Mommy-blogging not working out for you?"

I shook my head. "Too many duck-face selfies. It hurts my cheeks."

"You sure you qualify as an influencer?" she asked.

I bridled. "Of course. Just this week a city councillor blamed his troubles on 'conservative political forces and their agents in the corporate media.' That's me, a conservative political force."

She frowned. "I thought you were a pawn of the liberal elites."

I slapped my forehead. "It's so hard to keep my media conspiracies straight. Honestly, slip me fifty bucks and I'll say whatever you want."

This is the heart of influencer marketing: paying for opinion. Get somebody with a soapbox and pay them for their heartfelt endorsement of whatever you're selling, whether that be dish soap or democracy.

It used to be enough to get celebrities to do so in what was obviously somebody else's advertisement (BTW, Jell-O, what happened to those Bill Cosby commercials?), but now it's subtler, with the endorsement woven into the influencer's own brand, casually inserted among their other social media posts as though the sentiment were coming from the poster's innermost soul, not their wallet.

Herding your own personal flock of sheep earns good money too. In 2021, a company called Hopper HQ calculated that the social media posts of top celebrities, the ones whose Instagram followers outnumber the populations of big countries like Russia or Japan, could be worth more than $1 million apiece—meaning some could earn far more doing that than playing soccer, or acting, or whatever.

Note that $1 million for a single post is way higher than the entire $650,000 budget for the campaign in which those thirteen influencers were meant to prod more young people to vote. It's uncertain who you would get to split Elections Canada's kind of money. A Maple Leafs star? A Raptors bench-warmer? Somebody from *Schitt's Creek*? Me?

"Put me in, coach," I said. "I'll do it."

"You sure you're best positioned to sway Canada's youth?" she asked.

"Yes," I replied. "I'll do so by going in the other direction, telling them they needn't bother to vote."

This strategy capitalizes on my special gift: The anti-Midas touch. Whatever I endorse is immediately devalued. The hip factor of anything with which I associate myself automatically plunges by a good forty per cent. I'm pretty sure it was my adoption of the spiffy golf shirt-and-khakis combo that killed Sears as a fashion brand. Studio 54 went under after I ducked in to use the washroom. The owner of my bike shop implored me not to wear a riding kit bearing its logo; I agreed, for a fee. My form of influencer marketing is more like extortion.

This is the approach I will take with my Leave It to Dad campaign aimed at young Canadians, the idea being to alarm them into action.

"No need to cast a ballot," will be the message. "We Boomers will do it for you."

This will be conveyed through social media posts like:

- Don't worry about climate change and the terrifying loss of biodiversity. My generation has got it covered. Look, we banned plastic straws! #NoPlanetB #You'llProbablyBeFine #Don'tBuyWaterfront.
- Feeling so #blessed to have got into the housing market before they pulled up the drawbridge. Imagine paying 7.5 times your family income for a home. #Gratitude #I'veGotMine #StayOffOfMyLawn.
- So excited about the plan to bring back compulsory military service! For women too! #GenderEquality.

Just joking about that last one, Junior. Maybe.

Alas, Elections Canada eventually backed away from the $650,000 influencer idea. Maybe the agency decided it should just stay out of things and leave it to the parties to do their own influencing, to give young people reasons to get involved. That's the best way to motivate Canadians: give them something to vote for—or against.

A Traditional Christmas Outrage

IT WAS DARK AND deserted in the back of the school, away from the concert, which is why the lurking figure startled me.

"Jesus Christ!" I yelped, spilling my drink down my overcoat.

"How did you guess?" the man replied, slipping back into the shadows by the lockers.

I peered closer. He looked vaguely familiar: Long hair, beard. George Harrison? No, he's dead. "Pardon?" I said.

"How did you know I was Jesus Christ?"

I looked again. Of course! "You're wearing sunglasses, sandals, and a T-shirt that says 'I'm not Jesus,'" I said. "It ain't exactly Master of Disguise material."

"Sorry, I'm new to this," he said. "Never had to deny My existence before—at least, not since Stalin died."

"Why would You have to hide?" I asked, dabbing at my coat with a handkerchief.

"Oops," he said, ignoring the question and eyeing my empty glass. "That wasn't mulled wine, was it?"

"No, just water."

"Would you like it to be wine?"

"No, I'm good. Why are You in disguise?"

"Because I wanted to see the Christm . . . er, Winter Concert."

"So, come have a seat," I said. "The Grade 4s are about to sing 'I'm Dreaming of a White Day Before Boxing Day.' Too bad you missed 'We Wish You a Merry Blandly Generic Celebration of No Particular Significance.'"

"No," He said. "I'd best hang back here. I know when I'm not welcome."

"Of course you're welcome," I said. "It's Your birthday party."

"Not anymore," He replied. "Now I'm like the drunken uncle who embarrasses everybody at Giftmas dinner by dredging up uncomfortable family secrets."

"Oh, I'm sure that's not true," I said. "Let's go watch them sing 'Oh Come, All Ye Faithless.' It's real cute when the little ones toss their Bibles in the fireplace."

"Oh, for Dad's sake. They don't really do that, do they?"

"No, I'm just winding You up."

"Wouldn't put it past them," He sniffled. "Can't turn on the TV without somebody throwing around F-bombs like confetti, but try saying 'Christmas' and the Thought Police are all over you like tinsel on a tree."

"Shh," I said. "Not so loud."

Had to admit He had a point. To Big Brother, any suggestion that there may be room for Christ in Christmas is as offensive as a fart in church (apologies to anyone offended by the word "church"). From the Royal Canadian Mint infamously advertising "the 12 days of giving," to the TV spot in which a husband shouts, "Honey, get up, it's the twenty-fifth," to retailers instructing employees to say "Happy Holidays" instead of "Merry C-word," the past couple of decades have offered no shortage of stories about Big Brother shoving JC out of his own holiday.

Oh well, no point going on about it. The fuss over The Holiday That Must Not Be Named now feels like yesterday's battle, like the debates over the legalization of marijuana and Sunday shopping. Also, it appears a lot of that War on Christmas hysteria was overstated, anyway.

Still, we're always willing to get our backs up over a good Christmas Outrage, and not just those touching on religion. In fact, Christmas Outrages themselves have become an annual holiday tradition, just like turkey dinner, or carolling, or fistfights over the last parking spot at the mall. They're as much a part of the season as shortbread and short tempers.

They always follow the same pattern: A) somebody declares that some holiday practice that other people cherish is, in fact, offensive and B) this prompts a backlash that results in said somebody's chestnuts being roasted over an open fire.

Usually Christmas Outrages are triggered by people who, in true Canadian fashion, are not themselves offended but are acting on behalf of some theoretical others who could potentially feel slighted, though when you ask these potential offendees whether they are, in fact, in need of grief counselling, they look at you as though you have three heads.

One of the more recent Christmas Outrages has involved the classic 1940s duet "Baby, It's Cold Outside." Fans say the lyrics, a back-and-forth between a man and woman, are charmingly flirtatious, but critics say all they really flirt with is sexual assault. Some radio stations have stopped playing the song.

I don't know what to think, which is probably OK because nobody needs to hear another old guy weigh in anyway. I don't particularly like "Baby, It's Cold Outside" in the first place. Nor do I share the rest of the world's love of the movie *Elf*, in which Will Ferrell's Buddy innocently invades the women's locker room to sing the song with Zooey Deschanel while she's in the shower stall, which, gosh, hardly seems creepy at all.

I'm more concerned about the fuss over The Pogues' 1987 song "Fairytale of New York," yet another back-and-forth between a man and woman, which includes an earthy exchange in which Kirsty MacColl calls Shane MacGowan a scumbag, a maggot, and a word that rhymes with maggot. There's an online tug-of-war over whether the latter word's use in that context is homophobic, which jeez (and here I apologize to anyone offended by the vaguely religious "jeez"), I hope it isn't, because I love that song. Or maybe there is no context in which that term is acceptable.

We were also supposed to be upset about the 1964 animated-for-television version of *Rudolph the Red-Nosed Reindeer*. Although one poll identified it as the most beloved Christmas movie of all time, we also heard it was being condemned for Santa's "bullying" of Rudolph and Donner's failure to accept his red-nosed son. OK, it turns out these criticisms were all tongue-in-cheek, but that didn't stop news outlets from responding with indignant Christmas Outrage stories condemning the non-existent condemnation.

Me, I'm old-fashioned. I still like to save my Christmas Outrage for those who clip the wings of school play angels and censor the lyrics of (bleep)mas carols in pursuit of their goal of ensuring that the beliefs and traditions—Christmas trees, niqabs in government offices, whatever—of all Canadians are treated equally, which is to say suppressed like the Riel Rebellion. God (again, apologies) forbid that schools acknowledge that even though it is now largely a secular event, Christmas is still Christmas. Heaven (again, my bad) forbid that children should be allowed to ponder spirituality or values or the Big Questions, not when there are more important things to fill their minds— Kanye's divorce, say, or which influencer to emulate, or *The Old Man and the Sea.*

I was about halfway through this rant—my sputtering, purple-faced indignation having descended into a doubled-over-at-the-waist, gripping-my-knees coughing fit, right there in the back of the school—when I was interrupted.

Perhaps, it was suggested, I might want to set aside my Christmas Outrage and choose a different path to follow— maybe one involving peace on Earth and goodwill toward men.

Mrs. Dr. Romance

EVERY VALENTINE'S DAY, JACK KNOX surrenders his column space to Dr. Romance, who dispenses relationship advice to men. This year, however, the role is being assumed by Mrs. Dr. Romance.

Dear Mrs. Dr. Romance,
   How did you come to take over the advice column this year?
   Curious in Kamloops

Dear Curious,
   Well, there was this day when Dr. Romance kept interrupting Mrs. Dr. Romance to tell her how mansplaining really works. When Dr. Romance urged her to stop banging her head against the wall so that she could hear him better, she accidentally chopped off his typing fingers with a meat cleaver.

Dear Mrs. Dr. Romance,
   Are you sure you're up for this?
   Wary in Winnipeg

Dear Wary,
   Yes, like her husband, Lefty, Mrs. Dr. Romance is ready to cure heartache and write prescriptions for love.
Dear Mrs. Dr. Romance,
   I tried to impress my wife with an impromptu sexy dance, but when I peeled off my shirt she was all "What

are you doing?" and "Put that back on" and "You're going to get us thrown out of Best Buy."
Shirtless from Shawnigan

Dear Shirtless,
Women. Go figure.

Dear Mrs. Dr. Romance,
Bolen Books is holding a Singles Night tonight. I say to my girlfriend: "What kind of woman would be interested in a guy just because he reads boo . . . ," except when I look up, she's gone and her car is burning rubber down the road in the direction of the shopping mall.
Do you think she's going to the grocery to buy steaks for supper?
Vexed in Victoria

Dear Vexed,
I'm sure she'll be right back. Go wait outside by the barbecue. In the snow.

Dear Mrs. Dr. Romance,
I'm into hour nine of last week's Super Bowl coverage when she comes down from cleaning the gutters and rips the TV off the wall, throws it into the driveway, and backs over it with her car. "What are you doing?" I ask. "Crushing the patriarchy," she replies.
"No," I explain, "they're called the Patriots. I don't like them either, but don't you think you're overreacting?" (Women love it when you ask them that.)
She seemed a little wound up so I suggested she go for a walk, except I think she might have gotten lost because it has been five days and she hasn't been back. I'm getting hungry. Should I be worried?
Supperless in Saanich

Dear Supperless,

No, you're good. Go wait with Vexed.

Dear Mrs. Dr. Romance,

According to the latest census, Victoria has far more unattached women than unattached men. Should they change the name to Chicktoria?

Hilarious in the Highlands

Dear Hilarious,

Mrs. Dr. Romance prefers Paradise City.

Dear Mrs. Dr. Romance,

When I asked Dr. Romance if it was true that the fastest way to a man's heart is through his stomach, he replied, "Yes, but Mrs. Dr. Romance prefers to go straight in with a steak knife." Is this true?

Nonplussed in Nanaimo

Dear Nonplussed,

Mrs. Dr. Romance is a vegetarian. Got to use those steak knives for something.

So, that's your real answer to the what-do-men-want question?

No. The correct answer is "Who cares?"

Dear Mrs. Dr. Romance,

This Valentine's Day, the El Paso Zoo will name a cockroach after your ex and then feed it to a meerkat, which you can watch live on the zoo's Facebook stream. Does this not seem wrong?

Miffed in Montreal

Dear Miffed,

Absolutely. Why is it limited to an ex? Also, that reminds me of Willie Nelson's "All My Exes Live in Texas."

Dear Mrs. Dr. Romance,

No, you're thinking of another Texas country singer, George Strait. Willie Nelson is the hard-drinkin' cheater whose first wife sewed him into his bedsheets when he was asleep, then beat him with a broom handle.

Do you not see something wrong about that?
Concerned in Calgary

Dear Concerned,

Yes. How did he get a second wife (not to mention a third and fourth)?

Dear Mrs. Dr. Romance,

When I asked my lucky lady what she wanted for Valentine's, she said a special dinner would be nice— maybe tomato-basil bruschetta, followed by halibut confit with leeks, then crème brûlée.

I replied, "No, that will take you way too long to cook" (I'm thoughtful that way), but now I'm stuck for an alternative.

Last year's Thighmaster wasn't a big hit. I'm thinking of something to help her in the kitchen.

Any ideas?
Loverboy in Langford

Dear Loverboy,

A meat cleaver is always handy.

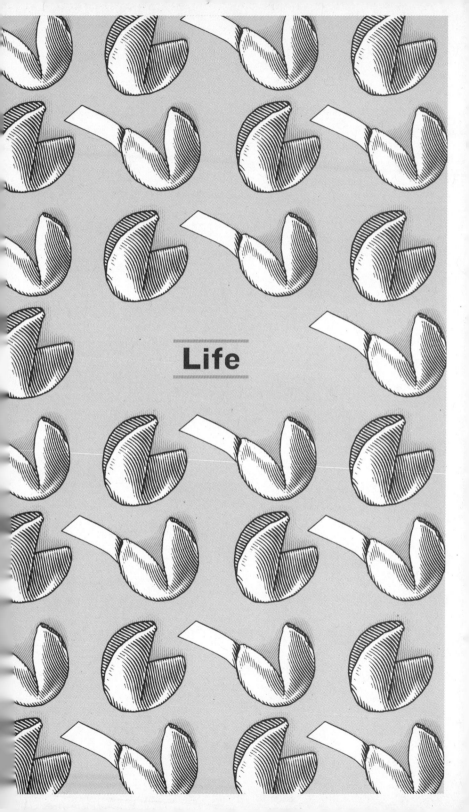

Life

The Big Picture

NEWS ITEM: Russian scientists will meet in secret to work on a plan for saving Earth from a possible catastrophic collision with a giant asteroid.

—Agence France-Presse

GOOD. **AFTER THAT, THEY** can figure out how to work my new television.

"It's the most beautiful thing I've ever seen," I said when we unboxed it this week.

"Ahem," she replied.

"It's the second-most beautiful thing I've ever seen," I said.

Our new television is the size of a small European country. It has its own area code. The remote control has more functions than the Elks Hall, is more complicated than Father's Day in Hollywood, and is harder to understand than an anti-vaxxer. So we didn't even try to do the techno-voodoo to bring it to life ourselves. Our teenaged friend Sam hooked it up last night, mostly, but it turns out we need another cable to make it fully functional. You always need another cable. You always need a Sam too.

Yet even in second gear, the new TV has, like Pavel Bure did in his first game for the Canucks, shown enough potential to make me excited about the future. I love the new television, take it for walks, buy it flowers.

My wife, on the other hand, just rocks back and forth with her arms pressed across her stomach, moaning, "It's too big, it's too big." I pointed out that there would be more space if she left the room, but apparently this was an error.

Our old TV was, well, old. The channel numbers came up in Roman numerals. It was coal-fired and had a "vertical hold" button, and when you turned it on, the news anchor wore a toga.

And it was small. To check the score of the game, I had to roll off the couch, toddle across the room, and invade the TV's personal space. "There's nothing wrong with my vision," I would say, eyebrows crackling with static electricity as I leaned into the screen. Foreign films with subtitles were out of the question.

We had our old television forever, were silently willing it to die, but it stubbornly clung to life like a dog wrapped around your leg, refusing to fade to black. So we finally just took the plunge, went out and caught up to the rest of the world, got the big screen 1080P 120 Hz with whitewalls, dilithium crystals, and whatever else our more modern friends insisted we needed.

"Join us," they chanted in unison, conjuring up memories of unblinking, pamphlet-wielding sidewalk cultists. "It will change your life."

"But I like the life I already have," I replied.

"No," they intoned, "your life is not good enough."

That's a sentiment we hear a lot, particularly as one year rolls into the next. As the calendar flips, we're urged to upgrade our lives like outdated iPhones. If Thanksgiving is about being grateful for what we have and who we are, New Year's resolutions are about feeling bad about what we don't have and who we aren't. Not thin enough, not fit enough, not bold enough, not rich enough, not enough toys. Not enough, period. It's one thing to set goals, to try to become a better person, but another to exist in a state of perpetual dissatisfaction. Resolutions are one part hope, two parts regret.

But here's the good news: The size of your TV—or bank account or ego—won't matter if the Apophis asteroid, 350 metres in diameter, comes flaming through your front window in 2036, creating a desert the size of France and killing hundreds of thousands of people, which is what those Russian scientists, meeting in 2010, feared might occur.

Here's even better news: Updated calculations by NASA's Center for Near-Earth Object Studies in 2021 found that such a collision is no longer in the cards. There is no risk of Apophis smacking into this planet for at least another century, if then. It now appears Apophis will do like the asteroid 2002 NN4, which got kind of close to us in June 2020 but then took one look, went "No, no, no, no, God, no," and decided to keep going. It locked the doors, stomped on the gas pedal, and, breathing a sigh of relief, fled our bad neighbourhood in search of a less pestilence-ridden planet.

And who knows? Maybe if we all work together, we can remove pestilence as a threat too. Now, that would be a great New Year's resolution. Of course, if we want high-definition resolution, we'll need Sam to hook it up.

When the Pen Was Mightier Than the Keyboard

I CANNOT WRITE.

Yes, you reply, that's obvious.

No, I mean that literally: I can no longer write longhand. I lost the ability years ago, probably around the time I lost my last comb or my Blockbuster Video card. On those rare occasions when I am forced to abandon my computer keyboard or my phone and pick up a pen instead, like a caveman, I print the letters individually, not cursively. Even then, the results come out in a chimp-fisted font best described as Early Ransom Note.

This is neither rare nor new. For many of us, longhand gave way to digital decades ago. As far back as 1999, letter writing—at least of the envelope-and-stamp variety—had declined so sharply that Canada Post launched an advertising campaign encouraging us to put pen to paper more often. "If somebody takes the time to sit down and write a letter, you know that effort went into it," a Canada Post spokeswoman was quoted as saying at the time. "Letters are truly a labour of love."

Yes, comes the reply today, that's why we stopped writing them. Why labour when you can just text two happy faces and a beer mug emoji? So imagine my surprise the other day when an envelope containing a five-page, single-spaced, handwritten letter landed on my desk.

"What are these squiggles?" asked the young colleague who opened it (she had done so at my request, as I had automatically assumed the envelope contained anthrax spores).

"It's called handwriting," I explained. "Just like texting, only with a three-day delay. In Ancient Greek."

OK, that's an exaggeration. They still teach both printing and longhand in BC schools, though it's no longer required that students conform to a standard style of penmanship. That frees them from the tyranny of the MacLean Method of Writing, a regimented style drilled into students across much of Canada for generations.

The MacLean Method was developed in Victoria in 1921 by H.B. MacLean, the first principal of George Jay Elementary, in response to teachers' complaints of sloppy handwriting by students. MacLean's method was so widely accepted (at its peak, it was used by schools in seven provinces) that when MacLean died in 1976, the *Vancouver Sun* marked his passing with an editorial published entirely in longhand. It was ingrained.

No more. Even if BC kids learn handwriting today, it's in the way their parents learned Grade 8 French. And if you're not using it outside the classroom, how deeply will it take root? A vigorous rear-guard action is still being fought, mind. The Saanich Fall Fair has a penmanship competition for young people. Advocates speak glowingly of the elegance and character imparted through cursive writing.

More important, perhaps, is what it means to the thought process. Most of what we get by email or text isn't writing, it's typing—unfiltered blather that pours out as fast as the fingers (or, now that we have voice-to-text, the tongue) can move.

Back in the olden days, the cumbersome nature of handwriting, the lack of a backspace key, forced people to take the time to really work out what they wanted to say before committing words to paper. Composition required care. ("I only made this letter longer because I had not the leisure to make it shorter," French mathematician and philosopher Blaise Pascal wrote in 1657.) Back in the olden days, you could tell when a writer had slaved over a letter: it came out of the envelope smelling like half a pack of Export A's.

Not now. Now, emboldened by the self-righteous certainty of the terminally ignorant, we post opinions—judgments, really—faster than we can digest the information needed to inform them. Maybe that would have happened in times of yore too (give ol' Blaise Wi-Fi and an iPad and he might have churned out 3:00 AM drunktweets about horse dewormer and a wall with Mexico), but we're not leaving a great legacy today.

That's what was impressive about my letter in the mail. It was well thought-out, logical, linear. It had obviously taken effort to write. It was a pleasure to receive. Which is why I replied with two happy faces and a beer mug emoji.

Fun for the Whole Family

CONGRATULATIONS! IF YOU ARE reading this owner's manual, it means you have just purchased and are ready to install your FunFamily home entertainment system.

This combination television, home theatre, music player, and gaming centre promises years of enjoyment—and that's just in hooking it up!

Before you start, read the entire manual and make sure all components are at hand. You'll also need AA batteries, a Mandarin–English dictionary, a bench vice, a pipe wrench, and a degree in electrical engineering.

STEP ONE: Insert batteries in remote control. Turn proudly to significant other, who should nod in an encouraging manner.

STEP TWO: Acquaint yourself with front of remote, which features more tiny buttons than a wedding dress. (HINT: Never depress the Code Set and Menu buttons at the same time, as this will cripple the electricity grid from Vancouver to Seattle.) Be aware that you will still need your old remotes too. (They're under the couch.)

STEP THREE: Connect the gaming console to the A/V receiver, following the colour-coded diagram on page 12. Be careful not to confuse the colours magenta, red, crimson, and scarlet. Shoo away family members who offer to help.

STEP FOUR: Connect the composite audio/video cable to the television.

STEP FIVE: You can stop looking now. The composite audio/video cable is not included in your FunFamily home entertainment package. Drive to the store and shell out another $40 to acquire one. (We warned you to read the whole manual before starting, didn't we?)

STEP SIX: Pick up small bottle of Valium on way home. You're going to need it.

STEP SEVEN: Enable pass-through via HDMI cables to A/V receiver and then outputs for 4K Ultra HD, 8K Ultra HD or Atari 2600 systems. (HINT: If you are old enough to remember the first Trudeau, then you should probably not attempt this installation alone. Instead, we recommend you acquire a teenager for this purpose. Be aware that the 2005 to 2009 models now come with AttitudePlus, available in Smirk, Eye Roll, or Amused Condescension.) Grumpily dismiss any other family members who offer assistance.

STEP EIGHT: Array speakers in optimal positions near your screen. Marvel at how small they are. Realize there are supposed to be six of them, not five. Locate missing speaker in laundry room, where it is being used as a door stop. (HINT: Your old beer-fridge-sized speakers from the last century can be gutted and used as garden boxes, or perhaps coffins for the next family member who offers to "help.")

STEP NINE: This next step is critical. Following directions precisely is very important, as failure to do so could result in complete system failure and the voiding of your warranty: Link MD/CD-R Out jacks to D-TV/CBL function by running digital link to input DTS bitstreams (acceptable for 96 kHz sampling) while jamming a salad fork in an electrical outlet and farting sparks.

Alternatively, you can bypass this process by simply pushing the big red button on the front of the tuner. (This option available in Singapore and Australia only.)

STEP TEN: Stomp down to basement, use bench vice and pipe wrench to disengage childproof lid from Valium container.

STEP ELEVEN: You are now ready to turn on your FunFamily home entertainment system. Press the power button on your remote control. If nothing happens, please turn to pages 367 to 524 of volume 4 of your FunFamily owner's manual for easy trouble-shooting tips.

STEP TWELVE: Plug it in, you moron.

STEP THIRTEEN: Still not working? Insert non-functioning components in 350° oven for 45 minutes, turning occasionally. Do not overcook. On second thought, do.

STEP FOURTEEN: Scour Mandarin–English dictionary for equivalent to phrases "shoddy workmanship," "outraged consumer," and "the horse you rode in on," then email well-reasoned letter of complaint to chairman of FunFamily parent company.

STEP FIFTEEN: Throttle family member who admits to "borrowing" batteries from remote control while you were in the basement with the Valium.

STEP SIXTEEN: Drive to Pennsylvania, abandon car, and join the Amish, swearing off all modern technology. Do not attempt to turn on radio en route.

Short Parkers, Unite!

"**N**OT BAD," I ADMITTED to the agent. Roomy, decent view, good area. It was ideal. I didn't want to appear too anxious to plunk down my money, though.

I checked out what my potential new neighbours were driving: Lexus sedan, Mercedes coupe. Nice.

"How much?"

"Three hundred a month."

Ouch. A little steep for a parking space, but you get what you pay for. Hmm, if I sold the house and moved into the trunk of the car, maybe I could swing it . . .

Just then an SUV wheeled into the adjacent spot. It was one of those new big ones, a cross between a large Humvee and a small Gulf Island. You know what I'm talking about: leather interior, touch-screen infotainment system, escalator to the driver's seat, helipad, crew of six.

"The deal's off," I declared and left in a huff (a 1965 Huff, with push-button automatic transmission). No way I was renting space beside that behemoth.

A statement of environmental outrage? Pshaw! You want to murder the Earth with a 2023 Gas Hog DL instead of a fuel-efficient 1997 Kyoto Accord, that's your business. Run over a whooping crane if you like, I don't care. Empty an aerosol spray can out the window while you're at it. (OK, not really.)

No, what gets my knickers in a twist is returning to the parking lot only to discover that my normal-sized car has been boxed in by a vehicle so massive that it blocked out the sun when it squeezed in beside me. It's like finding yourself docked in the lee of an aircraft carrier, one that renders you blind as you reverse out of the stall. Think of backing into a bar fight with a hood over your head.

The problem has worsened as vehicles have grown. The typical personal vehicle is now longer than a cricket match, higher than Seth Rogen, and wider than a salesman's smile.

And not only are big vehicles bigger, but there are more of them too. Marketing wizards say aging baby boomers feel more secure when surrounded by a lot of metal. (It used to be Black Sabbath, now it's a black Suburban.) By 2015, seven of the ten top-sellers in Canada were SUVs, vans or trucks, the latter built tough enough to haul logging equipment or a freshly killed moose through the rugged back roads of downtown Vancouver.

Compounding the challenge, while cars have bulked up, with side-impact safety features adding to their width, parking stalls haven't. Think of those stalls as your pre-pandemic jeans. The vehicles we drive have become too big for the spaces in which we park them.

Sometimes the gap between vehicles is so tight that you can't even open your door. That's the way it was on this day, when I found my car side-mirror-to-hubcap with the aforementioned SUV/Gulf Island whose wheels had inched over my side of the line the way the Russian army inched into Ukraine. The only way I was getting into my car was A) by losing the Christmas shortbread weight or B) squeezing through the sunroof. I don't have a sunroof.

As you might expect, parking-related insurance claims are way up. You would think this would spur the authorities to adopt what I believe to be a no-brainer solution: short-car-only parking spots. That is, just as there are handicapped and driver-with-baby stalls, there should be sections of parking lots reserved for regular-sized cars. This would solve the obscured-vision issue.

Now, signage alone wouldn't keep big vehicles out of these spaces, just as it doesn't keep them out of small-car-only slots (apparently some drivers define "small" as any vehicle without Gray Line Tours painted on the side). Builders would have to enforce the short-car rule with physical barriers—five-foot ceilings, head-high strands of barbed wire, perhaps the odd burst of gunfire to keep tall parkers on their toes, if not their backs. This would leave sedan drivers crawling out of their cars on their hands and knees, but I think they would still be on board with the idea. Enough is enough. Short parkers, it is time to rise up. Then duck down.

Of course, it would also help if people left their cars at home. You first.

Name Games

WHEN CRIMINAL CHARGES WERE laid against Donald Trump's campaign aide George Papadopoulos, another George Papadopoulos took to Twitter to protest that he was not that George Papadopoulos.

To which Michael Bolton (no, not that Michael Bolton) tweeted the reply, "I feel your pain, brother."

That, in turn, inspired James Taylor (no, not that James Taylor) to add, "We should record together, man."

And that led to John Ratzenberger (no, not the one from *Cheers*) to chime in with, "Maybe we should start our own support group."

Similarly, a Colorado radio host named Erin O'Toole woke up one morning in 2020 to discover that, unbeknown to her, she had become leader of the Conservative Party of Canada overnight. Or at least, she was getting messages from Canadians who had confused her Twitter account with that of the politician. When she pointed out that she was an American woman, not a Canadian man, someone responded with "But what do you think about Quebec dairy farmers and supply management?" Then Elizabeth May chimed in. No, not that Elizabeth May. The one who replied to O'Toole is a bestselling author who lives in Perthshire, Scotland, not the member of Parliament who lives on Vancouver Island. May the author could relate to O'Toole the radio host's predicament. "I've received entire angry e-mails . . . not for me," she wrote.

It must be weird to go through life like that, hauling around a name made famous by someone else. I'm not referring to monikers that are kill-your-parents punny from the outset, though there's no shortage of those. (My sister went to school with Pearl Arbour. I had neighbours named Jack, Peter, and Bunny Rabbit. Yes, there really was a man christened Drew Peacock.) Nor am I referring to names that you poison yourself. (The verb "bushusuru"—meaning to vomit violently in public—entered the Japanese language after George Bush Sr. famously chucked his cookies in the lap of Prime Minister Kiichi Miyazawa at a state banquet. There was even a popular nightclub act in which a trained monkey—not George Jr.—would hurl upon hearing the word.)

No, what we're talking about is when, out of the blue, your perfectly unremarkable name gets dragged into the spotlight (or the mud). Brad Pitt was just a guy in Haida Gwaii at one point. Ditto for Vancouver's Harry Potter. Same goes for Victoria's Michael Jackson. "People used to like doing 'Beat It' or 'Thriller,'" the latter man said. It was funny, oh, the first million times. After that it wore a bit thin. "I probably know something like 250 Michael Jackson jokes," he said.

At least Jackson didn't hear people cracking cannibalism jokes like Salt Spring Island's Mike Tyson did in 1997 after the same-named heavyweight boxer, apparently hungry for something more than victory, bit off half of Evander Holyfield's ear during a title fight. (The story took an odd twist when the Salt Spring Tyson discovered his Hawaiian hotel was next door to the one where Holyfield was staying. Fortunately, there was no rematch.)

Some people embrace the notoriety. The late Freddy Krueger, who drove the Victoria airport shuttle, used to dress up as the horror-movie character on Halloween. He even lived on Saanich's Elm Street at one point.

Alas, sometimes when Good Names Go Bad there's no such thing as grin and bear it. Sometimes a name becomes so toxic that you have to change it rather than suffer shame through association. Pre-war Canada had a liberal dusting of Mussolinis and Stalins, even an Austrian-born Hitler who immigrated here in 1905 (he was Jewish, by the way). You won't find them in the phone book today.

Likewise, during the First World War entire Canadian communities felt compelled to rebrand as something less German-sounding. Berlin, Ontario, became Kitchener. Dusseldorf, Alberta, was retitled Freedom. Prussia, Saskatchewan, not only changed its name to Leader but also dropped German street names in favour of numbers. Carlstadt, Alberta, was renamed Alderson after the British commander of the first Canadian division in Europe, which was a bit of a bummer for him in that the village soon became a ghost town anyway. Even the king wasn't exempt: In 1917, anti-German sentiment also led our Royal Family to ditch the House of Saxe-Coburg and Gotha in favour of the current House of Windsor.

More recently, some first names have taken on negative connotations. The once-popular John—the kind of name that mowed its lawn, paid its taxes on time, and helped old Beatrice across the street when her hip gave out—fell out of favour after becoming synonymous with men who frequent prostitutes. Half a century ago, 366 British Columbia babies were named John, but by 2020 there were just 56. As for poor Karen, she had fallen right off the page.

I would feel bad about all that if my own real name—John Knox—wasn't slang for venereal disease in certain parts of Scotland.

Game Names

WE'RE COMING UP ON a century since a West Coast* team has won the Stanley Cup.

The last ones to do it? The Victoria Cougars, who beat the Montreal Canadiens in 1925. Alas, after one more finals appearance in 1926—the Cougars lost to the Montreal Maroons—their league folded. The Victoria players moved to Detroit where, after a few years as the Cougars, they morphed into the Falcons and, ultimately, Red Wings.

West Coasters had to wait for the arrival of the Vancouver Canucks in 1970 before getting their hopes up again, though in retrospect that turned out to be like waiting for the *Hindenburg* to dock in New Jersey. Being a Canucks fan is like leaving the porch light on for Amelia Earhart.

Which brings us to today's topic: The Seattle Kraken is a stupid name.

That is, the latest NHL entry skated out in 2021 and promptly fell through the ice and sank to the bottom of the standings, which is what they deserved for choosing such a dopey name. Great Harold Ballard's ghost, could they have made a worse choice? FYI, a kraken is a mythical Scandinavian sea monster. It has nothing to do with Seattle or the Pacific Northwest, meaning that, right off the hop, the selection fails the first rule, which says a good team name reflects an aspect of its community. Think Edmonton Oilers, Brandon Wheat Kings, New Westminster Salmonbellies, Prince Rupert Rainmakers, or baseball's deliciously christened Nanaimo Bars.

Ideally, the owners of the Kraken would have followed the locally appropriate (not to mention alliterative) pattern set by soccer's Seattle Sounders (named for Puget Sound), basketball's Seattle SuperSonics (whose name came from the city's aircraft industry), and football's Seattle Seahawks (not a real bird, but close enough). But no, instead they had to come up with something that, within minutes of the announcement, had us awash in, er, wisekraks about fans known as Krakheads filling an arena known as the Krak Shack.

Not that the Seattle braintrust is alone in making unfortunate choices. Some picks have best-before dates. Toronto may love its Raptors, but the name seemed as outdated as Napster or parachute pants as soon as the *Jurassic Park*–inspired dinosaur craze faded. Same goes for the Anaheim Mighty Ducks, who came into being a year after the Disney movie of the same name (the word "Mighty" was dropped after Disney sold the team).

Anaheim wasn't the only one to tweak its name. In the 1990s, the owner of Washington's basketball franchise decided Bullets was no longer right for a city ravaged by violent crime, so changed it to Wizards. Baseball's Devil Rays became the supposedly less-satanic Rays. And how on earth could we have ever thought the name Washington Redskins was OK? It took until 2020 for it to disappear.

Other cases are less clear-cut. The Chicago Blackhawks argue their name honours an individual Indigenous leader. Do Seattle's historical hockey names—Thunderbirds and Totems—constitute cultural appropriation or regional pride? To stay on the side of the angels, the Edmonton Eskimos rebranded themselves Elks and the Cleveland Indians became the Guardians in 2021. The owner of hockey's Saanich Braves came to the same place without being shoved. Baseball's Atlanta Braves have not.

Deciding what to call a team is a delicate business. Schools now have to tiptoe around a long list of rules, which is why they often come up with something as blandly inoffensive as an airline magazine. Nothing nasty that conflicts with school values. No corporate names (remember the Bad News Bears, sponsored by Chico's Bail Bonds?). Gender and cultural issues are taken into account: Nicknames and mascots tied to a specific group cannot be adopted without consultation with that group, whether there are perceived negative connotations or not. (Would the Notre Dame Fighting Irish pass the sniff test today?)

It's not always easy to keep up to moving goalposts, though. What seems appropriate one day—smoking in airplanes, the strap, hipster man buns—can be anachronistic the next. In Langford, Belmont Secondary's boys' sports teams were called Braves and the girls' Tomahawks until 2000, when someone looked at the calendar and realized it wasn't 1950. A newspaper editorial at that time cheered the change, though not because it found the Braves and Tomahawks to be any more offensive or culturally inappropriate than all the cartoonish Highlanders and Vikings running around high school gyms in their more-Hollywood-than-history tartans and horned helmets. No, the editorial just wanted names that reflected something representative of the school or its area.

Note that the University of Victoria blew a golden opportunity in this regard when it wisely dropped the Vikings (no local relevance) and Vikettes (any name ending in "ettes" or starting in "Lady" is a non-starter) but replaced them with Vikes, a meaningless invention that sounds as though it should get excellent fuel economy. Couldn't they have picked something more indicative of Victoria, like Galloping Gardeners or Thundering Bureaucrats or Weed Kings?

You can only adopt such a local name when a team stays put, though. The Flames made sense for Atlanta, a city that was put to the torch in the Civil War (just like Vancouver when the Canucks lost to Boston!) but not when the franchise moved to Calgary. Ditto for when the Lakers departed Minnesota for Los Angeles. Likewise, Cougars was a good name for Victoria but not Detroit.

There has to be room for quirkiness, though. You can't help but have a soft spot for the old Victoria Salsa (nothing says Victoria like a Mexican condiment) junior hockey team owned by the same people who had Taco Time, or for the Castor Raiders (say it quickly) in Ed Bain's Alberta cattle country hometown. Also, three cheers for the Macon Whoopee of the old Central Hockey League and the Fighting Artichokes of Arizona's Scottsdale Community College.

Some of the best names don't actually exist at all. A CBC Radio contest in which listeners were invited to invent team names produced the Nitinat Paddywhacks, Port Simpson Homers, Port Melon Collies, and both the Metchosin Ones and the Metchosin Few.

When it comes to choosing names, some teams need to get kraken.

(*California teams don't count, because they have no business being in the NHL.)

My Apologies to the Thief

MY CAR WAS BROKEN into the other day. Don't know who did it, though it was parked right behind the premier's office—not that I'm necessarily suggesting anything.

It was just one of more than three thousand thefts from vehicles so far this year, many of which could be prevented if we didn't tempt thieves by leaving stealable stuff in plain sight.

So the break-in was, I now see, my fault. Just back from a trip out of town, I left my luggage on the front seat instead of stowing it in the trunk. Next thing you know, the bag was gone, replaced by a pile of broken window glass.

Since I'm to blame for the luggage being swiped, it must also be my fault that its contents were so unrewarding: shaving kit, running shoes, the new Janet Evanovich book, a ball of over-ripe laundry.

Must have been a dreadful disappointment to whoever stole the bag. My laundry isn't worth that much clean, let alone dirty. For this, I offer my heartfelt apologies to the thief. I can only hope that he at least enjoyed the book, which, ironically enough, involved a vehicle theft. Perhaps if the thief and I ever cross paths, he can tell me how the story ended.

It must also have been terribly difficult for the thief to get into my car, because he not only smashed the window but found it necessary to break the door lock too. For this unwarranted inconvenience, I am once again profoundly sorry.

I shall endeavour to do better in future and will make a point of leaving an iPad in the car, or maybe a phone, or a hand-gun. Actually, it's hard to tell what's popular these days, so I'm never quite sure what to leave out for the thieves. Perhaps a Starbucks card or a bottle of wine. New clothes are always good, but I never know what size to get, and it's really a matter of taste, isn't it? Of course, there's always money—it's a little crass and impersonal, but when it comes to practicality, there's nothing like cash. That, or some nice crystal meth, whipped up in the bathtub (homemade is always better, don't you think?)

Of course, it would be easier to pay for these goodies if I weren't already saddled with the cost of the last break-in. Not to be critical, but there's some wacky math at work here. I'm out about $300 to fix the car and maybe another $300 to replace the stolen bits. The thief, meanwhile, ends up with A) a book, B) half a tube of Crest toothpaste, and C) an assortment of unwashed dad clothes, the kind that make teenagers wince and maintain a 200-metre gap between themselves and their parents. Total resale value: $5.

This badly tilted expense-to-profit ratio isn't uncommon either. One of the two guys with whom I share an office had to pay $350 to fix his car after a thief broke in and stole a $47 power inverter. The other guy had his car burgled too, suffered $400 worth of damage, but the thief didn't get a thing, not even a dime hiding in a cupholder. Often as not, that's all the thieves want: the loose change.

In that case, why not just leave the doors open and put a sign in the window saying "Four quarters in the ashtray, help yourself." Your car could get raided three hundred times before the expense matched the insurance deductible from a single break-in.

In Vancouver, some drivers leave notes in the window saying, "Car open, no valuables inside." I briefly toyed with the notion of going the other way, leaving a duffel bag stuffed with half-crazed rottweilers in the back of a truck, sowing land mines and fang-toothed leghold traps around the perimeter, but was reminded that my break-in was my fault. I should have hidden the bag if I didn't want to be robbed and, in any event, I barely made it worth the thief's while.

Sorry.

Terms of Endearment

NEWS ITEM: In 2003, receptionists and security staff at city headquarters in Bristol, England, were told to stop calling members of the public "dear" or "love," and to address them as "sir" or "madam" instead.

The order came from Barbara Janke, the new leader of the city council, who said some visitors to city offices had objected to the informal way they were greeted.

—Independent on Sunday

NAME THREE. **C**OME ON, Barbara. (May I call you Barbara? Babs? Your Worship? The Jankemeister?) Name three people who genuinely got their bloomers in a bind upon being referred to as "dear." Do that and I'll name three people who should be banished from England.

Do not pass Go. Do not collect 200 quid. Drag their prissy, lemon-sucking, pucker-butted bodies on a plane and fly them to Purgatory—or worse, Toronto—where they can lead an existence as briskly businesslike as a prostate exam.

Just don't dispense with one of the most enduringly endearing facets of life in England, where 56 million people are sardined into a country just over four times the size of Vancouver Island yet still manage to treat one another as individuals.

We expect Canadians to be blandly distant, the French to be haughtily aloof, Americans to teeter wildly between gun-on-the-table, back-to-the-wall wariness and the alarming familiarity of a steakhouse waiter on ecstasy. But the English? They have always had the knack of being friendly without fawning.

I like it when they call me "love." It tickles me pink when grandmotherly publicans address me as "dear" or "darling" (or anything unrelated to anatomy). This has nothing to do with being flirtatious. "Dear" is a substitute for "buddy," not "baby." Love, dear, pet, treasure, mate. Even when they don't mean it, even when they utter it out of habit alone, it's cuter than a bucket of puppies.

It's not just England. In 1981, while entering a security checkpoint in Belfast, Northern Ireland, I blundered into the wrong line-up, not knowing there was one for men and another for women. My transgression drew the snarling attention of a red-faced, blue-uniformed woman who looked like Jason Momoa. "What the hell are you playing at, love?" she demanded.

"Nothing, honey buns," I replied.

Well, no, I didn't say that. If I want a rubber bullet in the teeth, I'll play hockey. Discretion being the better part of cowardice, I just mumbled an apology and slithered away.

Maybe I should have dazzled her with a uniquely Canadian term of endearment. Like "k'wala'yu," a Kwak'wala expression from the BC coast meaning "you're my reason for living." (Try it on your spouse some time. Mine responded with "Whatever.") Or I could have hauled out a little bit of Turkish: "ArkadasIm olmandan gurur duyuyorum ama hislerimizi karanlIkta saklamaktayIz." ("I'm proud that you are my friend, yet we are hiding our feelings in darkness . . . ") I bet that one would have tamed my wild Irish rose. Or maybe not. Wouldn't have wanted her to misinterpret my intentions. There's a time and place for everything, including breezy informality. (Let's not forget the Texas judge who habitually punctuated his signature with a happy face, which was a nice touch right up until the day he applied it to an execution warrant. I'm not making this up.)

Not only is there a time and place, there's also a who. When the Brits or the Irish start spreading the affectionate epithets, it's charming. When a Canadian tries it, it's an invitation to a restraining order. Let me call you sweetheart? No, better to stick with buddy, or pal, or partner (or even, if you must, the execrably Keanuish "dude"). But on the other side of the Atlantic, they can—and should—pull it off.

Forget formality, Mayor Barbara. Don't confuse impersonal officiousness with professionalism. Unleash the lexicon. Instead of banning the personal touch, make it mandatory.

Frankly, Barb, my little buttercup, cara mia, snookums, when I go into City Hall, I am less concerned with a lack of formality than an overabundance of bureaucracy. Never mind "sir" and "madam." Lower my property taxes and you can call me Zippy the One-Eyed Wonder Pig. Otherwise, at least give us a little love.

I Cannot Tell a Lie

"**THIS FOSSIL,**" **SAID RICHARD HEBDA,** not batting an eyelash, "is a colony of ancient barnacles from the Rocky Mountains."

And really, who was I to disagree? Hebda was a scientist at the Royal BC Museum, while my own grasp of natural history was as shaky as a Hollywood marriage.

Except that fossil turned out to be a sea cow tooth, didn't it? Hebda was lying. Ditto for archaeologist Martina Steffen, who prevaricated with conviction while passing off a whalebone harpoon as the target in an ancient ring-toss game.

In fact, the museum was full of fibbers for a good cause. This was Artifact or Artifiction, a fundraiser at which the experts talked about museum pieces and you had to decide if they were telling the truth or not. As it turned out, the best way to tell who was telling the truth was this: the liars were having more fun.

Which, despite the admonitions of priests and parents, is as it should be.

Lying has been given a bad rap. It is, as is the case with all good sins, both enjoyable and rewarding.

Imagine the calamities that would fall, the pleasures denied, if you were to tell the truth all the time: The dog didn't eat my homework. The cheque is not in the mail. Actually, those pants make your butt look enormous.

As a young man, I was quietly enjoying a glass of lunch in a London pub one day when it was suddenly invaded by a swarm of soccer hooligans. Massive buggers, all tattoos and muscles and rage, just like the bad guys from the Mad Max movies, except in black-and-white Newcastle United strip.

The other patrons wisely fled the pub screaming like little girls. Me, I stayed rooted in place, mesmerized by the sight of The World's Biggest Skinhead ordering a pint of whisky. "What you looking at?" he demanded in a barely decipherable Geordie accent, which is like Scottish, except twice as drunk.

"My grandfather was from Newcastle," I blurted. This was a lie, a total falsehood, not even within taxi distance of the truth. But, like a life preserver tossed in desperation from a sinking ship, it saved me from a horrible death.

Ignited by the spark of kinship, the massive skinhead became my new best friend. Hugging my shoulders tightly with one hand, absentmindedly crushing the skulls of stray Londoners with the other, he happily told me about life as a hooligan, how he and his mates would take the train to wherever Newcastle was playing each weekend, and either go to the game or get arrested first, didn't much matter to them—a point he emphasized upon leaving the pub, when he slapped the helmet off the head of one of the policemen who had been called to restore order.

The bobbies, after they finished bouncing their nightsticks off his noggin, chucked him in a police van. As they closed the doors, my newfound Newcastle cousin looked me in the eye and, with a river of blood tracing a Mississippi down his face, gave me a huge cheery grin and wave. True story.

The point is, had I just sat there like a tourist/victim ("Canadians: Just as punchable, but twice as polite!"), they would still be dragging the Thames for my body. Lying saved my neck. "Truly, to tell lies is not honourable; but when the truth entails tremendous ruin, to speak dishonourably is pardonable," Sophocles said.

This is what is known as a white lie—or, as I like to think of it, a good start. A white lie is a fib with training wheels, one that comes with an "N" in the back window. Having tasted the benefits of a flexible truth, the novice can progress to more daring, albeit justifiable, falsehoods: Claiming Chester Field as a dependent at income tax time, phoning in sick with the Friday flu, pretending to have given at the office. "A little inaccuracy sometimes saves tons of explanations," wrote the English satirist Saki (and that name was itself a lie, being the pseudonym of Hector Hugo Munro).

Pretty soon, you're on to the really good stuff: "I am not a crook." "I did not have sexual relations with that woman." "We hate the GST and will kill it." "As prime minister, I'll make sure the 2015 election will be the last under a first-past-the-post system." Of course, to lie at that level, one must first be elected.

Cats and Dogs

NEWS ITEM: A pet cat is being hailed a hero after saving a man from his burning home in Bracknell, England. As black smoke filled Andrew Williams' bungalow, his neighbour's cat Hugo came through a cat-flap and raised the alarm by clawing at the father-of-two's face.

—BBC News

PERSONALLY, I THINK HUGO was just coming in for the kill. Smelled the smoke, peeked inside, saw the homeowner wasn't moving, figured he'd snatch the guy's wallet before the fire finished him off. Just bad luck that Andrew woke up.

It was Hugo's own fault, really—guess he couldn't resist the urge to get in a couple of swipes while the man lay there defenceless. Next thing you know, a slightly sooty Andrew is sucking oxygen on the lawn and Hugo is being hailed as a hero cat, which is kind of like being a good Samaritan or bad Rotarian, the exception that runs counter to stereotype.

That is, cats aren't exactly famous for their selfless devotion to others. The concept of sacrifice is foreign to felines. They belong to the Me-ow Generation. You'd never see a cat take a bullet for the president.

True, the *Times Colonist*'s Carla Wilson once fielded a call from a reader who insisted that his cat had saved his life by leaping up and performing pussyfooted chest compressions during a heart attack (I'm not making this up), but this claim was written off as a touching, albeit frightening, case of self-delusion. (The guy probably spends his days sitting by the mailbox, waiting for the Nigerian general's cheque to arrive.) CPR? No, Fluffy was just frisking the shirt pockets for cigarettes.

Not, I should hasten to add, that I wish ill toward cats. No, I made the mistake of leaving that misconception in a column many years ago, and I am just now recovering from the blistering vitriol hurled my way in response. "A disgrace to the name human being," one letter writer called me. "Despicable," wrote another. "Disgusting." "Hateful." "Abhorrent." (I didn't even know Mother could spell "abhorrent.")

Therefore, to be perfectly clear, let me stress once again that I wish our feline friends no harm. They are just as God made them: pestilential, savage, cunning psychopaths, as dangerously unpredictable as Martha Stewart with half a gallon of sloe berry wine in her belly and a glue gun in her hand. Like rattlesnakes, scorpions, and Albertans, cats cannot be blamed for being what they are and should never be mistreated.

Cat owners, on the other hand, should be put down. What are they thinking? Cat owners are nothing but dog owners with a death wish. These must be the same people who golf in lightning storms and heckle Hells Angels at traffic lights. A cat is not a pet, it's a furry hand grenade, except that you can tell when a grenade is going to explode. One moment it's a contented kitty, happily horking up a hairball in your lap, and the next it's not just biting the hand the feeds it but taking off the entire arm.

But dogs! Well, the world is full of heartwarming tales of loyal labs and courageous collies charging to the rescue, pulling babies from the lake, taking on cougars, busting pool cues and backing up their owners in bar fights. Note that in 2021, the nominees for the American Humane Hero Dog Awards included three courageous canines that had made a living sniffing for explosives—though some might argue this career choice had less to do with the presence of bravery than the absence of intelligence.

Actually, Stanley Coren, a University of British Columbia psychology professor and author of several books on canine behaviour, did research showing that the smartest dogs have the mental ability of a two-and-a-half-year-old child (whereas the dumbest have the intelligence of a middle-aged husband). Dogs found among the canniest breeds—border collies, German shepherds, retrievers, poodles—have a vocabulary of about 250 words and signals, while the least intelligent—Pekingese, beagles, Afghans, Trump Republicans—spend a lot of time watching Fox News and "doing my own research." Dogs can also perform very simple math, which is more than you can say for the typical person.

Whether this makes dogs smarter than cats, I don't know—or care. Cat owners might dismiss dogs as servile beasts, but the attributes that we really cherish in a mutt—loyalty, friendliness, courage, unconditional love, the ability to remain poker-faced while breaking wind—are the same that we value in humans.

"The average dog is a nicer person than the average person," Andy Rooney once said. And affectionate? Every time you come home it's like being greeted by Jimmy Fallon on *The Tonight Show*. There should be theme music.

Perhaps that's why so many of our canine companions have human names. A book called *Move Over, Rover: What to Name Your Pup When the Ordinary Just Won't Do* lists the most popular choices for dogs, including Max, Molly, Sam, Lucy, Sadie, Cody, and a bunch of other names that sound like a Grade 11 roll call. My friend Andy Dunstan adopted a dog that he named Jack, mostly because it scratches itself in public and drinks from the toilet, which Andy said reminds him of someone.

But let's give cats their due. In England, they're saying Andrew Williams owes his life to one. He might want to check for his wallet, though.

Parable of the Lava Rocks

GOOD MORNING. TODAY'S LESSON is taken from the Parable of the Lava Rocks.

I bought the last bag of barbecue lava rocks at the store on Saturday. Was halfway to the car, my mind still dwelling on a variety of Kardashian-related checkout-counter headlines, before I realized the price at the till was twice what was listed on the shelf.

So I waddled back inside and stood quasi-patiently in the kind of long, snaking line normally associated with papal funerals or Disneyland until it was my turn to make wounded bleating noises to the pleasant, though harried, young woman at the counter.

After a certain amount of punching of computer keys and discussions with her headset, she solved the mystery: "You took these from the wrong shelf. These are the Mesquite-Tinged Gourmet Rocks With Flavour Action. You wanted the Flaming Roadkill Specials. The computer says we have fifty-four bags in stock."

She refrained from smirking and rolling her eyes, but muffled snorts of derision came from the shoppers stuck in line behind me. I hung my head, chastened. A man of simple tastes and simpler wallet, I had erred, selecting lava rocks above my station and, worse, wasting valuable service-desk time.

"Wait to the side and I'll send someone to fetch the right rocks," the clerk said magnanimously.

So I shuffled a few feet over to that special corner of service-desk purgatory reserved for those who have offended the shopping gods. The customers whose breath was moments before heating the back of my neck streamed past, sizing me up for a dunce cap with sidelong glances.

Several minutes passed. I shifted from foot to foot like a kid left holding his mother's purse in the lingerie department. Several more minutes passed. Outside, the sun was setting. Somewhere in the distance, a dog barked. Still no lava rocks. The stock boy appeared to have vanished into the vastness of the Big Box Bermuda Triangle. The clerk and I exchanged the uncomfortable half-smiles of two people sharing a long elevator ride.

Suddenly, her forehead knit in consternation. "But the computer says we have fifty-four bags," she told her headset. She was aghast, perplexed, her world turned upside down.

I did have the right shelf, she informed me, but it was now empty, which is what I had told her twenty minutes before. I felt vindicated, like the guy from *The Fugitive* after they nailed the one-armed man. I stood taller, prouder. The clerk looked at her shoes.

"The stock boy has gone to the back to look for lava rocks," she said. Or maybe he'd gone to Toronto, because several more minutes passed without any sign of him. He had disappeared—poof!—like Mel Gibson, the Tamagotchi craze, or an election promise.

I wish I could say I accepted all this gracefully, that I smiled indulgently, behaving toward the beleaguered clerk as I would hope she would behave were our roles reversed. "It is not your fault," I should have said, "that you are overworked and underpaid, that your employer has taken all the money that should have gone to hiring staff and has instead blown it on a defective inventory-monitoring system. You and I are just helpless passengers on this crazy merry-go-ground called life, our souls slowly being sucked away by the heartless, ineluctable realities of low-margin, high-volume commerce."

But I didn't. Instead, I waited for my lava rocks with ill grace, arms folded, nostrils flared, periodically glancing at my watch. I huffed and puffed like the bull on a Bugs Bunny cartoon, moaned and groaned like a porn movie, smouldered and steamed like a volcano, threatening to erupt and make my own lava rocks, right on the spot. I was, in short, a wiener.

"Oh, never mind," I grumbled eventually, wheeling and marching out of the store, overflowing with self-righteous indignation but totally lacking in lava rocks.

By the time I got to the car, my temperature had cooled. (It was, after all, nearing midnight.) I felt like going back to apologize. Instead, I pretended to get into a nearby SUV, just in case the clerk was watching, recording licence plate numbers and toying with the idea of impaling my tires—or, worse, me—with a barbecue fork. If she does, I hope she brings lava rocks too.

Pi Day

IT'S PI DAY TODAY. Sorry, I forgot to get you a card.

Now, giving a mathematical symbol its own day of honour may seem odd. But pi, as those who were sober in math class will remember (the rest of us may need a bit of refreshing), is one hot little number.

As William L. Schaaf wrote in *Nature and History of Pi*, "probably no symbol in mathematics has evoked as much mystery, romanticism, misconception and human interest as the number pi." Well, you can't deny that. How many times, while caught in traffic or a passionate embrace, have you found your mind drifting with the thought "What is pi, anyway?"

The answer, as most people—or at least those with pocket protectors—know, is that it is the ratio of a circle's circumference to its diameter, 3.14159.

That's why Pi Day is celebrated on March 14 at one minute to two in the afternoon—3:14:1:59. ("Celebrated" may be too strong a term, unless you consider changing the batteries in your calculator to be a form of expression.)

Coincidentally, March 14 is also Einstein's birthday, which gets Pi-heads all giddy, as though God did it on purpose. Michael Caine and Billy Crystal were born on this date too, but the math guys don't mention that.

Anyway, in the interest of science, it seemed an appropriate time to demystify the subject and answer a few of the math-related questions that have been keeping you awake at night, or perhaps putting you to sleep in class. Here goes:

Jack, how did man discover pi?

It was in the back of the fridge, behind the marmalade and the baking soda.

Is 3.14159 the entire number?

No, pi goes on forever, like Trump talking about election fraud. In 2002, a Japanese team calculated 1.2411 trillion digits of pi.

Can you think of any other never-ending numbers?

Yes, and they were all sung by Celine Dion.

What is the purpose of pi?

The purpose of pi is to highlight the inferiority of those of us who need twenty minutes to figure out the tip on a $12.69 lunch. A less sensitive commentator than myself might observe that the world can be divided into two groups—those who understand pi, and those who have personalities—but the pi people would dismiss that as jealousy. That, and they would audit my taxes.

Why is pi called an irrational number?

First, it says it wants to talk, then it makes you play Twenty Questions to find out why it's upset. It asks to be taken somewhere special on its birthday, then ends up fussing with its hair for an hour, so you miss the first period. It's calm one moment, then suddenly erupts in anger, demanding that you stop drinking out of the milk carton (at least in the grocery store). Really, there's no living with it.

Where did the name pi come from?

Pi is short for Pythagoras, the mathematician who discovered it.

Are you making that up?

Yes, but he did devise Pythagoras' theorem, which is that in a right-angle triangle, the square of the hypotenuse equals the sum of the squares of the adjacent sides.

What is a hypotenuse?
A large, water-dwelling mammal in Africa.

What other types of triangle are there?
Isosceles, scalene, equilateral, Bermuda, and love. The latter two are killers. That's a joke.

Do you have any other examples of mathematics humour?
Yes, try this knee-slapper:
> **Q**: Why is it so funny that the Japanese should calculate pi to 1.2411 trillion digits?
> **A**: Only forty-seven decimal places of pi would be sufficiently precise to inscribe a circle around the visible universe that doesn't deviate from perfect circularity by more than the distance across a single proton!

I'm telling you, there wasn't a dry seat in the house.

I am confused by the terms used in trigonometry. What is sine?
Pisces. What's yours? Can I buy you a drink?

No thanks. Do you know what happens when mathematicians drink too much?
Actually, I don't. What happens?
They get pi-eyed.

The Law of Attraction

"**D**ON'T FIRE ME BECAUSE I'm too hot," I told my boss.
"That won't be the reason," he replied.

I tried to hide my relief. I never saw my movie star looks and smouldering sexuality as a workplace liability before, but this Iowa case has changed things.

A court there ruled that it was OK for a dentist to fire his assistant of ten years for no other reason than that he found her an "irresistible attraction" and feared for his marriage.

To repeat: She hadn't done anything wrong. She hadn't pilfered the petty cash. Hadn't huffed the laughing gas. Hadn't even flirted with the boss who, being twenty years her senior, she saw as something of a father figure.

The dentist, on the other hand, found himself having urges, and said he was distracted when the thirty-two-year-old woman wore tight clothing. (Note to self: Get rid of pre-pandemic pants lest editor be driven mad with desire. He's hetero, but best not to take chances.) When the dentist's wife discovered he was exchanging text messages with his assistant, she urged him to fire the woman before friendship flamed into affair.

Now, some people might argue that the onus should have been on the employer to restrain himself, but hey, maybe there's something about the world of spit sinks and rubber dams that saddles its inhabitants with ineluctable impulses.

When we watched *Horrible Bosses*, in which Jennifer Aniston played a sexually aggressive dentist who preys on her assistant, we didn't know it was a documentary.

The thing is, when the Iowa assistant sued for discrimination, she lost. Even when the case was appealed, the all-male Iowa Supreme Court (state motto: Don't bump your pretty little head on that glass ceiling, honey) ruled in 2013 that the firing, while unfair, was based not on sexual discrimination but on the dentist's desire to save his marriage. The learned judges stopped short of actually awarding him a medal or naming a high school in his honour. At least they removed the "irresistible attraction" language from the ruling, clarifying that people are responsible for keeping a leash on their desires.

The Iowa court actually got a lot of support from legal experts. The complainant couldn't claim sexual harassment because, ironically, the boss fired her before doing anything untoward. Nor was she discriminated against as a result of her race, religion, or other status protected by law. Being "too hot" isn't on the list.

On the contrary, conventional wisdom holds that beauty is a workplace advantage. A Texas economics professor named Daniel S. Hamermesh, the author of a book titled *Beauty Pays*, even argued that since unattractive people make less money than good-looking ones, ugliness should be treated as a disability worthy of legal protection.

Now, we all know life is good to the good-looking. They get better jobs, better tables, better service. (True story: I was once in a McDonald's where the woman behind the counter gave my change to the only other customer, a Chris Hemsworth lookalike.) But this flip side of the coin, the idea that Big Brother should embrace the unhuggable, is relatively new.

"It's a matter of simple prejudice," wrote Hamermesh in a 2011 *New York Times* opinion piece. He cited a series of studies, including one that showed an American worker in the bottom one-seventh in looks, as judged by random observers, earns 10 to 15 per cent less than a similar worker whose looks were deemed to be in the top third.

His solution: "Why not offer legal protections to the ugly, as we do with racial, ethnic and religious minorities, women and handicapped individuals?" Because nobody likes to be called ugly, that's why. Because while there's little debate about who qualifies for membership in the other groups Hamermesh mentioned, pigeonholing the homely is a more delicate matter.

No one likes being judged, or at least being judged runner-up to Quasimodo. Back in the old days (because gosh, no one would act so unprofessionally now), I always dreaded stumbling into a game of Shag or Shoot, in which some of the women of the *Times Colonist* editorial department would debate whether they would rather A) sleep with a particular colleague or B) take a bullet. Alas, there were a lot of figurative shell casings on the floor. (Hey, it was a newsroom, not a firehall.)

The fact is, few of us are much to look at. And it can be argued that anyone who is not actually attractive is, by definition, unattractive. Jerry Seinfeld, in his eponymous television show, declared 90 to 95 per cent of the population to be "undateable." (Elaine: "Then how are all these people getting together?" Jerry: "Alcohol.")

But how would the authorities determine who is so hideous that the government has to step in? What are they supposed to do? Park us in a bar at closing time and see who bites? Run us in front of an *America's Got Talent*–type panel? Not sure I'd want Simon Cowell wincing, saying "Sorry, pal," and slipping me a $50 bill as compensation.

Besides, beauty, or the lack thereof, isn't the only basis for discrimination. Height matters, too. A Fortune 500 study found the average CEO stands six feet tall, looming three inches above the typical American man. The taller presidential candidate usually wins too. Before five-eleven-and-a-half Joe Biden, Americans hadn't elected a president under six feet since Jimmy Carter in 1976. Every prime minister since Pierre Trudeau, who at a relatively runty five feet nine was as tall as the average Canadian man, has been at least six feet tall. Justin Trudeau is six feet two. (Also, you might have noticed that few of those CEOs, and none of the elected presidents and prime ministers, have been female—but that's a whole other story. Or book.) On it goes. Some are born rich, others poor. Some have a great sense of humour, while others are Albertan. Some places make sense, while others are Iowa.

Nobody said life is fair. Inequities abound, so you might as well get on with what you've got. And that's the ugly truth.

The Tango Taliban

NEWS ITEM: Students in Port Angeles, Washington, are boycotting high school dances because of rules known as "Face to Face, Leave Some Space."

    The rules not only require students to leave a visible gap between one another when slow dancing, but ban back-to-front dancing, which school officials said could lead to inappropriate grinding.

—Associated Press

THIS RAISES TWO IMMEDIATE questions: A) what would appropriate grinding look like, and B) where's Kevin Bacon when you need him?

Apparently Vancouver Island's 'Merican neighbours across the Strait of Juan de Fuca need a little *Footloose* action, someone to offer up an empty grist mill just over the county line where the kids can bump and grind, or at least grind, away from the prying eyes of the Tango Taliban.

According to the *Peninsula Daily News*, Port Angeles High cancelled its 2013 Spring Fling after only fifteen tickets sold. Dozens walked out of class to protest the new rules, and the annual homecoming dance fizzled. Student representatives complained the new decree even meant no conga line or bunny hop.

This is not just a Port Angeles issue. The face-to-face edict is being enforced in schools throughout the US because, gosh, there's no threat, real or imagined, that the land of the free can't regulate into submission. In fairness to school authorities, though, they're trying to deal with a relatively new challenge. In the olden days, we didn't have to contend with back-to-front dancing (or, as it was called back then, "sexual assault"). Nor was there a need for the "leave some space" rule, since the space was generally from one side of the gym to the other, girls and boys propping up opposite walls. Every once in a while some poor gormless dweeb would gather the nerve to cross the great divide to ask the prettiest girl in school to dance, she would scrape him off the bottom of her shoe, and he would make the lonely, humiliating, three-day hike back across the floor, the band playing "Smoke on the Water" as a funeral march. The boy would then guzzle a smuggled mickey of lemon gin before becoming violently ill on the basketball court, passing into blissful unconsciousness after a few minutes of the dry heaves. This was known as "having a great time."

When couples eventually did hit the floor, the result bore less resemblance to *Dirty Dancing* than *The Walking Dead*, a self-conscious zombie shuffle, with the exception of the occasional kid energetically bopping away like Mick Jagger, or at least what Mick would look like should someone toss a toaster in his bathtub.

Then the band would play "Stairway to Heaven" and the girls would avoid eye contact. ("It's like a bear. Pretend you're dead and he'll go away.")

Of course, every once in a while a couple would not only dance cheek to cheek (as opposed to crotch to cheek) but cross the line between waltzing and making out, leading the teachers to wade in and pull them apart like linesmen breaking up a hockey fight. Back-to-front dancing might be relatively new, but teenage lust is not. If Port Angeles school trustees are fretting, it might be because of their own memories of "Paradise by the Dashboard Light." Or maybe the face-to-face rules really do reflect an assumption that today's youth are even more lecherous than they were (when adults use the phrase "today's youth," it usually comes with a scowl).

They might consider emulating those school districts where students are governed not by blanket rules that treat them all like sex-crazed rottweilers keen to mount the letter carrier the moment you let them off the leash, but by a general code of conduct that boils down to showing respect for others. This does not mean high school dances become porn movies. It means you cannot micro-manage kids to either safety or wisdom. Rather than smothering them in bubble wrap, installing surveillance cameras, using GPS trackers to monitor their driving habits or forcing them to dance stiff-armed as a von Trapp, how about imparting good values and trusting them to make smart choices on their own?

Of course, there are always chastity belts.

Language, Please

THE BBC THINKS I should put down my pitchfork.

Or, to be precise, a BBC.com opinion piece has—as a surprising number of my regular readers alerted me gleefully—branded me a language zealot.

The column, posted on the British news site, was about people who are a tad too eager to impale those who break the often arbitrary rules of English usage. I was herded into a pack of such pedants.

"Those who take up these weapons often use them viciously," wrote the piece's author, James Harbeck. "In his recent book *Bad English*, the language scholar Ammon Shea has collected some striking examples. One George Quinn, in a letter to the *Providence Journal* newspaper, said that a particular writer who started a sentence with a conjunction should have been 'appropriately beaten in grammar class.' The poet Phyllis McGinley said the sentence adverb 'hopefully' 'is an abomination and its adherents should be lynched.' Jack Knox, a columnist for the *Prince George Citizen*, advocated capital punishment for anyone who used 'gift' as a verb."

Prince George Citizen? OK, technically true in that the newspaper did reprint the column in question, but still a bit off base, like describing Hitler as a corporal in the Bavarian army.

As for the assertion itself: Guilty as charged. The line came from a column in which I urged the death penalty for anyone who A) wears a Speedo that he can't see for his gut, B) tosses cigarette butts out the car window, C) signals a left turn only after stopping at the intersection, D) TALKS! LIKE! THIS! on a mobile phone in a restaurant or, yes, E) uses the words "impact," "transition," "medal," "parent," or "gift" as a verb.

More to the point, I remain defiant. The verb "gift" (as in "I had an extra kidney, so gifted her one") impacts me negatively. It's an affectation, like making a show of carrying your yoga mat or pretending to like quinoa. Hang 'em high, I say.

Never mind that, technically speaking, I am flat-out wrong. As Shea argues in his 2014 book, "gift" has been used as a verb for more than four hundred years. Such usage eventually fell out of favour but was made popular again recently (kind of like Johnny Cash before he died).

Also, never mind that for me (I?) to moan about improper use of English is more than a little pot-kettleish, given the frequency with which more-qualified language cops bust me for driving without due care and attention. ("Shame on you!" chided one reader after I identified the two dots in Michaëlle Jean's name as an umlaut instead of a diaeresis, which I thought was what you got after eating an umlaut made with rotten eggs.)

Indeed, newspaper writers in general are to language what road salt is to an undercarriage. I worked with one reporter who wrote of a "bonified" hockey player (who had, apparently, been filleted) and another who referred to the Strait of Wanda Fuca (presumably the first woman to swim across to Washington). My paper once ran this photo cutline: "Above, Mary Smith prepares her vegetables before being baked in the oven." My boss once killed a reporter who repeatedly confused "it's" with "its," though we were encouraged not to reveal this. So, people who live in glass houses and all that.

But hey, if rabid anti-vaxxers can substitute "your sheeple" for "you're sheeple" on their signs, and if Donald Trump can tweet "I am honered to serve you" as he did on his first full day as president, then I can self-righteously point an accusing finger at those who butcher the English language, even while holding a meat cleaver in my other hand. At least I don't try to justificiciate my abuseling of the English language, as Sarah Palin did when she called on Muslims to "refudiate" plans to build a mosque near New York's Ground Zero. Apparently she was aiming for either "repudiate" or "refute" but crash-landed somewhere in the middle. When it was pointed out that there ain't no such entry in her *Funking Wagnalls*, she tweeted that "English is a living language. Shakespeare liked to coin new words too. Got to celebrate it!" Except when Shakespeare made up a new word, he did it on purpose, whereas Palin simply drove off the linguistic cliff, then tried to claim that she was going four-wheeling.

In truth, most of us don't have a firm grip on the wheel any more (anymore?). The evidence is everywhere. Texting has reduced us to digital grunting ("Where r u" or worse, "Wear r u"), while responsibility for proper spelling has been handed off to that drunken babysitter autocorrect. The gymnastics involved in avoiding the use of gender ("the driver who hit me took off without leaving their name") can result in awkward sprains, if not broken syntax.

Punctuation is a problem. We either forget to use apostrophes (mens room, indeed) or scatter them at random, as though playing pin the tail on the donkey. Ditto for commas. (Had I known the difference between "you never call me" and "you, never call me," I could have avoided a nasty restraining order.) Our "use" of "quotation marks" is more "arbitrary" than logical.

Words are wielded imprecisely. Pet peeve: The interchangeable use of "suspect" and "bad guy" in crime stories, even though the whole reason for using the former is to make a distinction between the criminal who is known to have committed the crime and the person who is—wait for it—suspected of being the criminal. When the TV news reported that pig-mask-wearing "suspects" fled through the garage after robbing Las Vegas's Bellagio, I repeated this point to my television screen at length until it was suggested that the news anchor might hear me better if I shouted louder. This could have been sarcasm.

It also brings us back to the whole point of the BBC article, which is that having language puritans running around in tall black hats with big buckles, burning heretics at the stake, is counterproductive. Caring about language usage is fine, but heaping abuse on those who err or deviate from the norm is—and here I paraphrase—buttheadish.

Guilty, your honer.

Catrimony

NEWS ITEM: A German man has unofficially married his cat after the animal fell ill and vets told him it might not live much longer.

Uwe Mitzscherlich, thirty-nine, paid an actress $400 to officiate at the ceremony, as marrying an animal is illegal in Germany.

Mr. Mitzscherlich said he had wanted to tie the knot before his asthmatic cat Cecilia died. The cat and groom have lived together for ten years.

—BBC News

WELL, **THAT HAS TO** be the wackiest story of the month. I mean, date a cat, sure, but marry one? Cats aren't really the marrying kind. Aloof, distant, all the loyalty and affection of a Katanga Secession mercenary. Not exactly the type of partner/pet you would want to take home to mother.

True, it would be handy to have a spouse who kills rats, but do you really want one who horks up hairballs, eats the goldfish, or triggers your allergies like a field of freshly mown ragweed? Better to wed a dog. At least Rover won't shred your calves like coleslaw if you try to use him as a footwarmer in the middle of the night.

There is precedent for this animal husbandry/wifery. Extensive research, or perhaps thirty seconds on Google, shows Herr Mitzscherlich isn't the first to say "I do" (or perhaps "I mew") to a member of the animal kingdom. There was a forty-one-year-old British woman who in 2005 married a dolphin in a ceremony sealed not just with a kiss, but a nice piece of herring. "It's not a perverted thing. I do love this dolphin. He's the love of my life," the Associated Press quoted the bride as saying of her decision.

In 2007, an Indian man wed a dog, hoping to break a curse he had suffered since killing two canines fifteen years earlier. In 1998, a number of television stations refused to air the *Jerry Springer* episode titled "I Married a Horse." I stumbled across—but really, really, really didn't want to delve into—a website called Marryyourpet.com. And, of course, about 10 million Canadian women have married pigs.

Besides, inter-species splicings are not so strange when compared to the phenomenon known as objectum sexuality, in which people, mostly women, fall for inanimate things. Britain's *Telegraph* carried the 2009 story of a US church organist who planned to marry an amusement park ride, even changing her last name to Weber after the manufacturer of the contraption she had ridden three thousand times. "I love him as much as women love their husbands, and know we'll be together forever," she was quoted as saying.

The *Independent* (why is it always British papers?) told the story of a San Francisco woman (why is it always Americans?) who took the name of the Eiffel Tower after wedding the monument in a ceremony in Paris (where else?) in front of a group of friends (hers, we assume) in 2007. She must go for the tall, silent type.

Then there was the Korean man who wed a pillow. And the Swedish woman who claimed in 2008 to have been hitched to the Berlin Wall for twenty-nine years. (She must have been devastated by the fall of communism.) And the Japanese guy who travelled to Guam to marry a Nintendo video game character. At least his bride was a depiction of a human, which, compared to the rest of the list, puts him in Cleaver/Waltons territory.

Now, having myself been accused of being an inanimate object, particularly when there are chores to be done but the Seahawks are on TV, I hesitate to criticize.

And I try to stifle any suspicions about the German guy who married his mouser on her death bed (sounds like a cross between *Love Story* and *The Incredible Journey*), even though the cynic in me still wonders if all this wasn't just a crude attempt to cash in on the cat's life insurance or pension benefits.

But really, what kind of relationship is it when only one party gets a say? Did anyone ask the cat/Eiffel Tower what they thought about being shotgunned into an arranged marriage outside their species/building code?

Marriage should be a two-way (or, if you live in certain rural areas, five- or six-way) affair in which both spouses bring something to the table but neither scratches the furniture.

The Bald-Faced Truth

I **HAVE GROWN A MOVEMBER** moustache.

You wouldn't know it because of the face mask, which I have been encouraged to keep on, but she's a beauty.

OK, I was hoping for a Ted Lasso/Burt Reynolds, dark and dense as Nordic noir, but what came in was more of an Aging Train Robber, like Bill Miner—another masked man, which is still cool—apart from an unfortunate patch in the middle that, from a distance, makes me look as though I want to invade Poland in search of a little lebensraum.

Others don't like my moustache as much as I do. Co-workers avert their eyes with a combination of embarrassment and revulsion, as though I have a booger stuck to my lip. One friend, normally as inscrutable as a poker player, blanched and took the Lord's name in vain. My wife has begun referring to me as her first husband.

Those reactions probably reflect the relative rarity of moustaches today. Forty, fifty years ago, everybody had a moustache: Elliott Gould in *M*A*S*H*, Tom Selleck in *Magnum P.I.*, Carl Weathers in *Rocky* (and before that as a BC Lion), Lanny McDonald, Frank Zappa, Hulk Hogan, Freddie Mercury, Lech Walesa, Harold Snepts, the Village People, your mother-in-law.

Indeed, history is full of famous soup-strainers: Albert Einstein, Salvador Dalí, Wyatt Earp, Martin Luther King, Clark Gable, and both Karl and Groucho Marx. Even Gandhi had a non-violent lip ornament. Nietzsche looked like someone glued a cocker spaniel to his face. Think of it as the equivalent of body art in a time when only sailors and convicts had tattoos.

Not today. People don't trust moustaches today. Canadians have grown to associate them with bad guys who are up to something sinister: Hitler, Stalin, Saddam Hussein, Snidely Whiplash, your mother-in-law. We might cover ourselves in more ink than a drunken pressman and sport more piercings than a knife fight, but we're wary of lip whiskers. Image-conscious politicians know this. It's no coincidence that Canada hasn't had a prime minister with a moustache since Robert Borden more than a century ago. (Bearded Trudeau doesn't count.)

These days, men either go clean-shaven or look like hairy lumberjacks (or at least what hairy lumberjacks would look like if they worked in the gaming industry). Someone suggested I, too, go back to a full beard, though when I shaved off the last one a pretty woman told me, "Losing your beard made you look a lot younger." That made me blush and squirm until she added, "Uglier, but a lot younger." Someone else suggested I grow chia hair or try some of that spray-on stuff for the top of my head.

But I digress. The point I was trying to make was that— Ted Lasso aside—moustaches aren't as in style as they once were. You could probably say that of Movember too. A dozen years ago there were all sorts of guys sprouting facial hair in the name of men's health. A whole bunch of us did so at my office, which was fun in the way that it's fun to plant a garden and see what comes up. Mike Devlin, already hairier than a bar brawl, ended up resembling a Doobie Brother, while Jeff Bell still looked boyish even though he was ninety-seven years old. Some had to weed the garden first: we had a copy editor named Bob who prepared for Movember by shaving for the first time since the 1980s. Not even he knew what he looked like under a beard that measured somewhere between Russian Revolutionary and Angry God on the Bristlemeter. One of the guys grew a moustache so luxurious that he fell in love with it, taking it for long walks in the moonlight and buying it jewellery. Couldn't blame him, because it really was magnificent. Yosemite Sam called to ask for an autograph. Canada Post gave it its own postal code. School groups touring the newspaper stopped to take pictures.

Such Movember efforts don't seem as common now, though Colin Newell, who leads a fundraising team at the University of Victoria, says we need them more than ever, because the pandemic has strained mental health. Guys tend to retreat and isolate themselves in a dark place when under strain, so it's important to both talk and listen to one another when needed, he says. "The difference between not coping and thriving can often come down to a conversation." It sounds like something the moustachioed Ted Lasso, the kindest character on television, might say.

Alas, while Lasso's 'tache might remain, I have been told I want to shave mine on December 1, quite possibly at one minute after midnight.

Clocking Out

I STOPPED BY THE INDIGENOUS school on the Saanich Peninsula the other day. A teacher was using an old-style analogue clock—a round one with hour and minute hands—to show Grade 2s how to tell time in the SENĆOŦEN language.

She told them how to say seven o'clock. It sounded like "tso-qus teentun."

"Tsoqus teentun," the children echoed in reply.

Then came 7:15, which sounded (sort of) like "tsoqus ee opun eeuks lkachus."

"Oh wow, that's a lot," blurted out a boy—but he still got it.

"Seems like the language might survive after all," I murmured to the guy next to me.

"Yeah," he replied, "but I'm not sure about that clock."

Point taken. How often do you see an analogue clock anymore? Most gave way to digital devices decades ago. Which was reinforced later in the day when the car radio reported that British schools are removing analogue clocks from classroom walls because teenagers—and here I paraphrase—are too stupid to use them.

Well, no, that story was later modified—slightly—to say that some British teachers are replacing analogue clocks because students, flummoxed by the whole big-hand/little-hand thing, keep interrupting exams to ask how much time they have left.

"The current generation aren't as good at reading the traditional clock face as older generations," a teachers' union rep was quoted as saying.

This was, of course, thrilling news to those of us who like to think of young people as human versions of JPEG photos, declining in quality with each generation. "Kids today couldn't pour beer from a boot with instructions on the heel," we grumble happily. Never mind that we do this while waiting for the kid in the computer store to retrieve all the family photos that we somehow erased (again) while trying to pay the BC Hydro bill online. We don't let a little thing like our own befuddlement ("Can I use the Cloud on a sunny day?") get in the way of our self-righteousness.

People love stories about other people's ignorance. It lets us feel superior. That's why we lap up headlines such as "Four in five Oklahoma City students can't read clocks" (a story that somehow didn't get as much play as its British cousin) and "Memorial University professor says students can't find continents on a map."

There is, in fact, a whole "can't find [fill in the blank] on a map" trope in which students are belittled for their geographic confusion. In 2002, with US troops fighting in Afghanistan, it was gleefully reported that only 17 percent of young American adults could find that country on a map. Likewise, in 2006, with American troops stuck in a war in the Middle East, the CBS News headline was "Where's Iraq? Young adults don't know."

A few years ago, when Donald Trump and North Korea's Kim Jong-un were waving their missiles at each other, Jimmy Kimmel sent a camera to the streets and asked young Americans to find North Korea on a map. They couldn't. Three pointed to Canada, which made us feel both smug and alarmed at the same time.

Canadians revel in US ignorance. "Harvard University students can't name Canada's capital," crowed CTV News in 2013. Over on the CBC, Rick Mercer used to have a recurring segment on *This Hour Has 22 Minutes* called "Talking to Americans" that was based solely on their lack of knowledge of their Great White Neighbour. Mercer suckered Ivy League students into condemning the Toronto polar bear hunt, and persuaded New Yorkers to praise our supposed achievements: "Congratulations, Canada, on eight hundred miles of paved road!" In 2001, a one-hour *Talking to Americans* show pulled 2.7 million viewers, a record for a CBC comedy special.

Not that we're exactly a nation of Rhodes scholars ourselves. "More than half of Canadians don't know how the prime minister is elected, and just 24 per cent can correctly name our head of state (it's the Queen)," Marc and Craig Kielburger tut-tutted in a (pre-WE Charity controversy) column. "Four in 10 Canadians cannot name our first prime minister or identify the year of Confederation," chimed in the *Globe and Mail*, making six in ten of us feel pretty awesome.

Maybe we should take the time (not necessarily on an analogue clock) to consider why we need the failings of others to feel better about ourselves.

Digital Detox

THEY'RE IMPROVING CELL PHONE service along the highway to Port Renfrew, and I am broken-hearted.

This is selfish, I know. The road to the tiny community, one of the remoter outposts clinging to the edge of Vancouver Island, is long and occasionally desolate. Logic says breathing life into the dead zones along the route is a good thing, particularly on that sketchy roller-coaster stretch where the guardrail graffiti used to read "HANG ON TO YER BEER!" as the pavement threatened to sling you into the Strait of Juan de Fuca. Safety first.

Nonetheless, word of the impending upgrades made me sad. Why? Because it means one less place to slip the electronic leash. I mean, for years, the high point of any Vancouver Island road trip was always that place—north of Campbell River, say—where cell service suddenly disappeared—poof!—just like Stephen Harper or the ice-bucket challenge. If you really had to connect, you could swing down into Sayward and, hanging off the porch of the recreation centre with one hand and doing the Statue of Liberty with the other, maybe find one bar of service, but otherwise you couldn't contact anyone and, more importantly, they couldn't contact you. That's when the vacation really began.

Not that I don't love my phone. I do. Maybe too much.

I spend more time with my phone than anyone else in my life. We go to work together, where our relationship is all business. We go shopping together, comparing prices. At home, we watch hockey side by side on the couch. "I hate to say it, but the Leafs look good," I'll tell her, which she'll confirm by spitting out a bunch of stats about Auston Matthews.

Sometimes, we'll go for a nice walk on the beach, just the two of us, gazing wistfully across the strait at Washington state until my phone blurts out a "Welcome to AT&T" message, which for much of the pandemic was as close to international travel as we could get.

We also bicker like an old couple, which is what we are. "Yes, I heard you the first time," I grumble when, impatiently, my phone sends me a second text alert. Not that there are many second alerts, so accustomed have we all become to leaping up like Pavlov's dog whenever our phones snap their fingers, demanding attention.

Our hypersensitivity to such demands might be at the root of something known as "phantom vibration syndrome," in which you feel your phone going off in your pocket even when it isn't there. In an article on Healthing.ca, a fellow named Nick Beare wrote that with almost 90 percent of Canadians owning a smartphone, this phenomenon (which he said is also known by the wonderful term "fauxcellarm") is quite common.

Of course, I wouldn't know what phantom phone syndrome feels like, because my phone is always there, unless I forget it. It's easy to know when people have forgotten their phones, because they'll suddenly sit bolt upright and tell you so: "I think I forgot my phone." Then, after slapping their pockets like an astronaut who just realized he left his smokes on Earth, they'll say it again, except panicked this time, like the mother in *Home Alone*: "Kevin!" (Some people name their phones.)

Reams have been written about the psychology behind this, about our craving for constant connectivity, or FOMO, or our addiction to stimulation. It's like a fork in a light socket. We can't let go. That has been particularly true during the pandemic, where one of the ironies is the way inertia and torpor have been fostered by constant anxiety and distraction. So much information piles in, all of it demanding our immediate attention, that we have trouble getting anything done at all.

As I write this, we're in the middle of a glorious spring, the trees raining pink blossoms, but I bet most of us barely notice because we're so deep in the weeds in our dissection of, say, the efficacy rate of Moderna versus Pfizer against the latest variant that the sun can't penetrate at all.

It has been suggested that this is unhealthy, that my phone and I, just like Ross and Rachel on *Friends*, need to go on a break. Sure, I reply, you go first. Easier said than done.

Which is why the enforced digital detox of a cell service dead zone was always such a source of both anxiety and relief.

Promises, Promises

"Broken promises don't upset me. I just think: 'Why did
they believe me?'"

—Jack Handey, *Deep Thoughts*

"**R**EAD MY LIPS, NO new taxes," promised George Bush the
Elder in 1988, and Americans made him president.

In 1993, Jean Chrétien successfully campaigned on a vow to
kill the Goods and Services Tax. You might have noticed that it's
still breathing.

Pierre Trudeau got elected in 1974 by promising no wage
and price controls, then brought them in anyway.

Stephen Harper called an early election in 2008, despite
promising to not call one until 2009, as mandated by his own
fixed-date election law. He won anyway, as did Trudeau Jr.
when he pulled the same stunt in 2021. Justin Trudeau had
come to power in 2015 after telling us straight-faced (though
not black-faced) that that year's election would be Canada's last
under a first-past-the-post system. It wasn't.

You might be shocked to learn that politicians break promises now and then. Income tax, Canadians were told, would
disappear after the First World War.

Land expropriated in the Second World War was supposed
to be given back, though the last time I looked, the Esquimalt
naval base was still sitting on the old village site.

In truth, most political promises do get kept, and when they
do go unfulfilled, it's often reality, not duplicity, that is to blame.
After the 1993 election, for example, it fell to Victoria's David
Anderson, as federal revenue minister, to convince Chrétien
that while the prime minister might have vowed to kill the GST,

impartial analysis showed Canada would be better off with a stay of execution. Chrétien agreed, knowingly taking the hit to his own reputation.

Still, there are plenty of promises of the "yeah, baby, I'll respect you in the morning" variety, vote-getters that are as forgotten as soon as the ballot boxes are emptied. It's the flimsy ones that make for great satire, that lead the parody parties—the obviously tongue-in-cheek, screwball outfits like Sweden's Donald Duck Party, Australia's Deadly Serious Party, or Mad Max Bernier's People's Party of Canada (what, it's not a parody party?)—to present outlandish campaign come-ons of their own.

Canada's Parti Rhinocéros Party, for example, promised to repeal the law of gravity, count the Thousand Islands to ensure none were missing, and breed a mosquito that would only hatch in January so that "the little buggers will freeze to death."

Frequent French presidential candidate Ferdinand Lop vowed to move Paris to the countryside so residents could breathe fresh air. (When the Nazis raided one of Lop's meetings during the Second World War, he clambered out a window declaring, "We do not retreat. We advance backward for strategic purposes.") Britain's Official Monster Raving Loony Party proposed reducing class sizes by "standing kids closer together," a suggestion that would give parents kittens during the pandemic. (Speaking of kittens, in 1999 the Loonies chose as leader a house cat named Catmando, whose promising career was abbreviated by a car tire in 2002, leading the party to call for cat crossings at all major roads.)

Really, the parody parties have the proper approach. If you can't keep your word, then at least make your word entertaining. Were I running (for office, not exercise, though both are highly unlikely) I would promise to:

- Bring back the lash, but only for those who are mean to BC's provincial health officer, Dr. Bonnie Henry.
- Ban overworked pandemic terms: A $40 fine for saying "pivot," "the new normal," or "in these

unprecedented times." The fine would rise to $400 for spelling it "unpresidented."

- Bring in a $75 fine for wearing your mask under your chin, $50 for covering your mouth but not your nose, and $25 for using it as an emergency coffee filter.
- Compensate anyone still waiting after their elective surgery was bumped by COVID-19. After languishing for three months, they should get a free burger and fries* on BC Ferries. After six months, their local elected representatives should have to do chores around their home. After a year, a geographical feature should be named in their honour. (*Not for heart patients.)
- Make Trudeau 2.0 apologize for apologizing all the time.
- Require anyone breaking the "nine items or less" rule at the grocery store to pay $5 per excess item to each customer in line.
- Require grocery stores to change the "nine items or less" signs to the grammatically correct "nine items or fewer."
- Make it punishable to wear a mask while committing a serious crime but also punishable not to do so.
- On second thought, I would also apply the lash to people who say "nucular" or "Febuary."
- Ban formal wear. Read my lips: No new tuxes.

Turning 100

MY MOTHER TURNS ONE hundred years old today, totally screwing up my retirement-budget calculations.

I put her longevity down to stubbornness. She never was a quitter, except when it came to cigarettes. (She once paid a hypnotist to help her stop smoking. It didn't work but she couldn't stomach the idea of wasting the money, so she went cold turkey.)

Or maybe we should credit her internal strength. She might have lost her mobility, much of her hearing, most of her eyesight, and, occasionally, her teeth, but she retains her ability to laugh, particularly at herself. A brittle person couldn't do that. When COVID-19 nudged her beloved little brother out the door, we feared the loss might be the end of her, but no, she soldiered on. Her response shouldn't have been a surprise, given what she told me a few years ago after I, reluctantly, passed on some heartbreaking news that I thought might buckle her. "Listen," she said. "There will be half a dozen times in life when you'll be blindsided by something so painful that it brings you to your knees. You won't think you will ever get up again. But you will."

She should know. She arrived just as the Spanish flu pandemic finally petered out, having killed maybe 50 million people over a two-year span—far more than were killed by COVID-19 during the same time span, and at a point when the global population was a quarter of what it is today. Her birth came exactly four years to the day after four machine gun bullets left her father half-dead in the blood and mud of the Somme during the First World War. He survived and went on to a life as a Canadian National Railway locomotive engineer (as children, my mother would admonish us to hold our noses whenever we crossed tracks belonging to the rival Canadian Pacific), but he always had what was referred to as a game leg that required ongoing operations.

Her family bounced around Alberta chasing work during a decade-long Great Depression that began when she was eight years old, and a world war that broke out just as she turned nineteen. She still talks of those friends who marched off, never to return—or to come back invalided to the Calgary hospital where she volunteered. In those days, mothers would run inside their houses, slam the doors, and draw the drapes when the telegram man appeared on the street, such was the fear of getting one of those dreaded "Regret to advise that your son ..." messages from the military.

The post-war world brought stability, but never prosperity (though not having much gave her empathy for those with even less). Nor was motherhood always the dream she imagined. There was the discovery of her drunken teenage son face down in the driveway in the traditional bracing-for-an-earthquake position one 3:00 AM. He might also have mooned the diners while strolling past the Highlander Restaurant, not knowing there were family members—and their friends—inside. I like to think these experiences helped her build character.

My sisters, who would prefer to remain anonymous but are Betty Jakel and Maggie Knox of Kamloops, also contributed. They would wait until Mum was seated in a washroom stall at Woodward's department store, ask her a question that demanded a long answer, then quietly back out the door so that the next woman to enter would be treated to a rambling monologue from the lone crackpot in cubicle three.

Mum gave as good as she got, though, retaliating by sending us to school with sandwiches with wax paper hidden inside, or by driving like Vin Diesel, causing some of us to lose our hair early. In her 90s, as her visiting children exited her home, she would stand in her window and feebly warble, "Don't leeeaaave me," which would cause passersby to glare at us reprovingly— and filled her with joy.

Today, we'll gather outside that window, as pandemic protocols require, and bellow at her over the phone. If we're lucky, she'll take those teeth out to recite "She sell seashells by the seashore," just to alarm/entertain the great-grandchildren. Fun, but hardly the celebration turning one hundred deserves.

One hundred years! On the day she was born, Babe Ruth got a hit for the New York Yankees. Mainland BC had eight kilometres of paved highway. The province was holding a plebiscite on whether to end Prohibition. Canada had 300,000 automobiles, as compared to 36 million today. Ballpoint pens, credit cards, sunglasses, bubble gum, and the sale of sliced bread were all in the future. She was born the year before Amelia Earhart began taking flying lessons.

Mum has not seemed particularly fazed by the pandemic. While it might overwhelm those of us who have lived free of real—or at least generational—adversity, to her it's just another crisis. Think six months of being locked inside with Netflix is hard? Try six years of war. Try losing most of those you have ever loved.

That's her hundred-year lesson. If she can endure, so can we.

Judging

PART ONE

PRETTY SURE I'M GOING to get shanked with a pie fork today. Someone on one of the Metchosin Day hayrides will spot my lifeless form splayed out behind the pen where they do the sheep-shearing demonstrations. "Any witnesses?" the cops will ask, and the beer garden crowd will just shrug, even though everybody will know who did it: one of the also-rans from the baking contest.

I didn't pause to think when I was invited to judge the baking event at this year's fair. Asking me to eat pie is like asking Snoop Dogg if he'd mind pulling a shift at Weed-R-Us. Several years ago the newspaper ran a letter to the editor from a man who declared the chicken-fried steak at My Chosen Café, just down from the Metchosin Day grounds, to be so good that "my current partner for life accused me of making noises normally associated with reproduction." That's how I feel about pie.

Except when I told people I was helping judge baking today, they blanched. Some crossed themselves. You fool, they said, you're going to make a few people really happy for a day and make fifty enemies for life—however short that life may now be.

For this is the truth: Country fairs, with their cow-pattie bingo, zucchini races, and Smart Car–sized pumpkins, are a ton of fun—right up until the judging, when you can cut the tension (if not all of the cakes) with a knife. That's when, with year-long bragging rights on the line, all the winemakers and calf breeders and canners hold bated breath as some high priest of the rural arts, with the grim-lipped intensity of an Amsterdam diamond-cutter, jams his or her nose into their entries in search of whatever it is that sets two jars of peach preserves apart.

This is serious business. I once made the mistake of innocently asking a Stetsoned man at Armstrong's Interior Provincial Exhibition how one goes about judging hay bales. "With bullshit!" he stormed, as his wife tugged anxiously at the sleeve of his jean jacket. "They judge them with bullshit!" Seems he had come third in alfalfa, or whatever.

Judges themselves can be baled a tad too tightly. My friend Debi Dempsey was thrilled after being awarded second place in a Saanich Fair pickle-making contest, but then grew curious after learning she had been the only entrant. Asked to explain the result, the judge drew herself up and replied, "They just didn't have first-place taste. They were second-place pickles."

But baking, baking takes the cake (as it were). Maybe it's the weight of a secret recipe handed down generation to generation like a family heirloom, the ingredients guarded as vigilantly as nuclear launch codes, but the pressure can drive people to extremes. Note that the winner of the 2014 Kentucky State Fair's buttermilk pie contest was stripped of her blue ribbon after it was discovered she had used a store-bought crust.

Also note the 1994 report of twenty-two people being injured in a melee that broke out after the winner of a Christchurch, New Zealand, baking contest was found to have bought her pie from a bakery. Unfortunately, this report was in the *Weekly World News*, a publication largely devoted to sightings of Elvis and Bigfoot, so is of uncertain veracity. Still, it's a good story, so I would like to believe it, even if no one at a Christchurch newspaper I contacted could corroborate it.

And let's not forget the scandal that rocked the UK's most-loved television show, *The Great British Bake Off*, when one contestant accidentally used another's custard, then 'fessed up after realizing what she had done. OK, as scandals go it wasn't exactly porn star Stormy Daniels getting paid off by the Pillsbury President, but if you mention Custardgate to the Brits, they'll know what you're talking about.

Not, I should hasten to add, that I would want to see baking contests disappear. Country fairs have already lost many of the traditional elements that, like your uncle cracking cringeworthy jokes at a family reunion, are now deemed anachronistic and inappropriate: chicken-plucking races, kissing booths, lawyer lynchings. The rodeo held alongside the Luxton Fair rode off into the sunset in 2014. Saturna Island's Canada Day barbecue no longer features a pig-diapering contest. The *Times Colonist*'s business editor, Darron Kloster, gets misty-eyed with nostalgia when recalling his hometown fair, where the farm folk of Abandoned Tractor, Saskatchewan, or whatever it's called, were urged to guess the weight of the fattest guy in town.

Also—and I cannot emphasize this enough—I like pie.

In summation: Dead man walking. It's been a slice.

Judging

PART TWO

JUDGED A COOKIE CONTEST once, a charity fundraiser. Sat in the sunshine nibbling baking with television's lovely Astrid Braunschmidt. Tough work, I know, but I'm kind of selfless that way.

Only one problem: We were looking for the Tastiest Healthy Cookie.

With all due respect to the organizers (not to mention the bakers), that's like searching for the fastest fat guy or the funniest Albertan. You can have totally healthy or totally tasty, but you can't have both. Saying "that's pretty good for a healthy cookie" is like saying "not bad for a Canadian sitcom."

Admittedly, asking me to judge healthy food is like asking Greta Thunberg to race NASCAR. When scanning packaging, I prefer ingredients that read like a Grade 9 science experiment, tending to categorize the likes of sodium nitrite and potassium bromate as comfort foods. Forget homemade. I like my cookies baked by Union Carbide or Dow. They should have the half-life of enriched uranium, more preservatives than King Tut.

Alas, there were no chemical-laced concoctions at Cookies For A Cause, as the event, a fundraiser by provincial government employees, was known. Propylene glycol alginate out, flaxseed in. And nuts. Plenty of seeds and nuts. One cookie appeared to have been made entirely of ingredients scavenged from the bottom of a bird feeder.

"Try it," Astrid said.

"No."

"It's for the kids."

"I hate the kids."

Another entry boasted of using carob as a substitute for chocolate.

"But I don't want a substitute for chocolate," pouted Astrid, no doubt voicing a sentiment felt by millions, or perhaps billions, worldwide. Substituting carob for chocolate is like Van Halen replacing David Lee Roth with Sammy Hagar—safer, but far less enjoyable.

And there's the rub: The lo-cal alternatives pushed by the Food Police (usually perky women in Lululemon gear) rarely taste as good as the evils they replace. While most of the cookie contest entries were surprisingly good, they were still not as addictive as, say, chocolate chip, the crack cocaine of confectionery. People eat chocolate chip cookies because they like them; no self-respecting stoner rifles the cupboards for carob after smoking a joint.

Government, in an attempt to make us change our eating habits, has spent years trying to persuade us that healthy tastes better. Yet no matter how often we try to convince ourselves that nutritious food doesn't remind us of compost, it's the smell of bacon, not broccoli, that makes people's mouths water.

Even politicians recognize this. Here's what George Bush had to say back in 1990: "I do not like broccoli, and I haven't liked it since I was a little kid and my mother made me eat it. And I'm president of the United States, and I'm not going to eat any more broccoli." Angry farmers reacted by sending Bush tonnes of broccoli, which was then given to Washington-area food banks, which is why poor people hate Republicans. Bush caught hell, but he was just being honest. But then, so were all those health experts when they warned of the consequence of our lousy lifestyle choices. We're getting fatter, wolfing down deep-fried diabetes even when we know it's bad for us, sending not only ourselves but also our children to early graves with pre-packaged heart disease.

Ah, but what to do? It would help if I were more nutritionally literate. I understand the broad strokes: anything that tastes bad is good, and anything that tastes good is bad. And I know I should eat more fruits and vegetables. We're also told that just as there's beer that's good for you (at hockey games) and beer that's bad (in church), there are good fats and bad fats. Non-hydrogenated canola oil is good, whereas pipeline-clogging trans fats are extracted from the Alberta oilsands, which makes them bad. Wo Fat, the gangster on *Hawaii Five-O*, was also bad, while olive oil is good, as befits Popeye's goilfriend. Anything more complicated than that, though, and this healthy-eating business becomes confusing.

Take the nutrition labels on packaged food. They list calories and core nutrients such as cholesterol, fibre, salt, pepper, bandwidth, and kilopascals, but what are you supposed to do with that information? "Look," my wife will say, "this box has 140 milligrams of polyunsaturated naughahyde," and I'll try to look serious and nod my head as though I understand what she's saying, just like your dog when you tell it to stay off the couch, but she might as well be speaking Martian.

Frankly, if you cruise the aisles in the grocery store, the only people you see reading the packages are those women in Lululemon pants. The rest of us are clueless. Health Canada needs to simplify things: Make food packaging carry warnings similar to those on cigarette packages, except instead of a photo of a smoker with some ghastly ailment, use a picture of an overweight guy in spandex.

Just don't touch my chocolate chip cookies.

The Meat of the Matter

As THE PAST COUPLE of stories show, I get asked to adjudicate a lot of food. Other journalists cover courts, or crime, or politics. I cover my tie with mustard.

"Jack Knox lives to give," I said, licking a stray piece of pork off the front of my shirt after staggering home from Ribfest. "The sacrifices I make for others are staggering. They should give me a medal."

She looked unimpressed. "How did you get barbecue sauce on the back of your neck?" Her reaction was not unexpected. I anticipate something similar when we go to the Metchosin Day fall fair. I actually persuaded her to stay for the fair's lamb supper one year (she had salmon), but then the farmer who raised the lamb pointed to my plate and said, "That's Buttercup," and suddenly we had to go home.

I turned my attention from my shirt. "You'd probably be more fun if you ate red meat," I told her helpfully. This earned me a scowl, proving my point.

This is what carnivores do. They try to get others to eat meat too. Sometimes, like the guy who spikes the punch bowl at the wedding reception, they'll slip a bit of beef into a vegetarian's meal, then sit there with a secret smile until it's consumed before disclosing their trickery. They seem to expect gratitude, as though one taste of the good stuff will hook the vegetarian like a trout (mmmm, trout) and shake them out of their wrong-headedness. They're surprised when, instead, the non-meat-eater comes at them with (ironically) a steak knife.

Likewise, some vegetarians like to dupe carnivores, waiting until the latter are done devouring the lasagna before revealing that it was made with eggplant, tofu, or some other form of compost.

They expect a Paul-on-the-road-to-Damascus conversion, as though the meat-eater will jump up and declare "WTF! I've been wasting my life on pulled pork when I could have been eating quinoa?" Regular readers of my column might recall that several years ago the People for the Ethical Treatment of Animals dared me to consume the meat-substitute Tofurky, a challenge I accepted in accordance with the First Rule of Journalism (always eat free food), though I kept a Big Mac at hand in case of an allergic reaction. I survived, but ended up spending Christmas in Victoria General with a burst appendix a mere three weeks later. (The doctors refused to connect the dots, but I figure that was just a liability thing.)

In any case, PETA's attempt to turn me was no more successful than its 2009 bid to have Victoria name its new sewage-treatment plant after Stephen Harper until "Canada's prime minister finally washes the blood of baby seals from his hands." (I'm not making this up.) Where I grew up, being a vegetarian wasn't a lifestyle choice. It just meant you were a lousy shot (though I do draw the line at the fast-food restaurant with the unfortunately worded sign "Our secret ingredient is our people").

So yes, when asked to judge Ribfest, I was only happy to accept. (Ribfest actually asked me to be a judge last year too, but I was already committed to MC-ing a fundraiser at a yoga studio because, gosh, Jack and yoga go together like Mother Teresa and hockey fights. I did get to use a stolen yoga joke, though. Me: Can you teach me those yoga poses? Yoga instructor: It depends. How flexible are you? Me: I can't do Tuesdays.)

But here's the deal: Whether you choose to eat cows, kale, or stuff that looks like it has been peeled off a truck tire is none of my business. So why do people feel compelled to lure one another to the other side of the grocery store? It's like that in many aspects of life—politics, religion, fashion, whether to cheer for the Leafs or a real hockey team—but nowhere in Victoria is the divide as acute as it is between those who think bacon is a vegetable and those who think it makes sense to airlift stray Victoria bunnies to new forever homes in Texas (which actually happened).

It's something to chew on, anyway (preferably with barbecue sauce).

Fashion Fixation

KATE MIDDLETON, THE DUCHESS of Cambridge, was in the news this week—or at least, her clothes were.

She was photographed in Aldershot, England, decked out in green while at a ceremony with the Irish Guards on St. Patrick's Day. Don't know what she said to the soldiers, because all the photo caption told us was, "Kate is wearing a coat by Laura Green and a hat by Lock and Co."

Apparently this is her life, the world paying more attention to what she wears than what she says or does. She could bark out, "I have a cure for COVID," or "I knifed a man in Lancashire," and no one would pay attention. Or if they did, it would only be because she triggered a run on orange jumpsuits.

Remember when she and Prince William visited BC in 2016? Shortly after their plane touched down in Victoria, a functionary rushed in front of the assembled media to breathlessly announce, "She's wearing Jenny Packham." Everybody else scribbled this down as though it were vital information, so I wrote it down too, though what seemed more remarkable was how Kate, with the cameras and the Trudeaus watching from the tarmac below, managed to descend the steep stairs from the RCAF Airbus in stiletto heels, Princess Charlotte in her arms, without taking a YouTube-quality face plant.

But no, what Britain's *Daily Mail* decided was headline-worthy was this: "Kate Middleton wins round one of outfit war with Canada's First Lady." (We have a first lady? There's an outfit war?) This fashion fixation continued throughout the week-long tour. When the royals were dropped into the breathtaking, wild beauty of BC's central coast, *People* magazine had eyes only for the duchess's boots, along with "a Holland and Holland jacket, her go-to Zara jeans and earrings by Canadian designer Pippa Small." Likewise, ABC News found Kate's "striking Carolina Herrera coat" more inspiring than the Yukon splendour in which she wore it.

Even *The Times*, its serious-journalism roots going all the way back to 1785, couldn't resist weighing in on its website: "Plain red dresses do not generally make headlines, even when they're worn by the Duchess of Cambridge. Yet the dress she wore this week to a dinner at Government House in Victoria, British Columbia, was not just any red dress. It's the best dress she's worn since the day she got married. It's possibly the best red dress in the history of red dresses."

Now, forgive me if I'm being overly sensitive about this, but as a fashion icon like the duchess, I do grow weary of having the public focus so heavily on my admittedly stunning appearance.

I can't count the times I have done something super-interesting (really, the story of how my appendix burst can drag on for a solid forty-five minutes) only to have the subsequent news report reduced to something like "Jack was wearing jeans that, while ill-fitting, cost just $16 during Boxing Week, a deal that he will still gush about to anyone who will listen."

While it's understandable that my adoring/envious public would yearn to know what label I, as an influencer, am wearing (FYI: probably Zellers, or something donated to Value Village by a dead guy's family), it does trivialize one, the implicit message being that the wrapping paper is more fascinating than the gift inside. Being objectified like that can be wearisome.

Sometimes people will gawk at the mustard stain on my 2003 *Times Colonist* 10K shirt and I'll have to say, "My eyes are up here, pal."

True, apparel can be part of a story. If you're the Canadian prime minister and swan around India dressed like an extra in a Bollywood wedding scene, or if you're wearing a hijacked Canadian flag, a F*CK Trudeau T-shirt, and a MAGA hat topped by a tinfoil protective dome, it counts as telling detail.

Yet sometimes such references serve only to distract from the meat of the matter. Shortly after the Russian invasion, Volodymyr Zelenskyy addressed the US Congress while wearing a military-green tee, prompting American financial commentator Peter Schiff to tweet, "I understand times are hard, but doesn't the President of the Ukraine own a suit?" This may have said more about Schiff, a guy who looks like he polishes his Guccis before wearing them to bed, than it did about Zelenskyy. Read the room, Peter. Or the planet.

Style matters, but don't forget the substance.

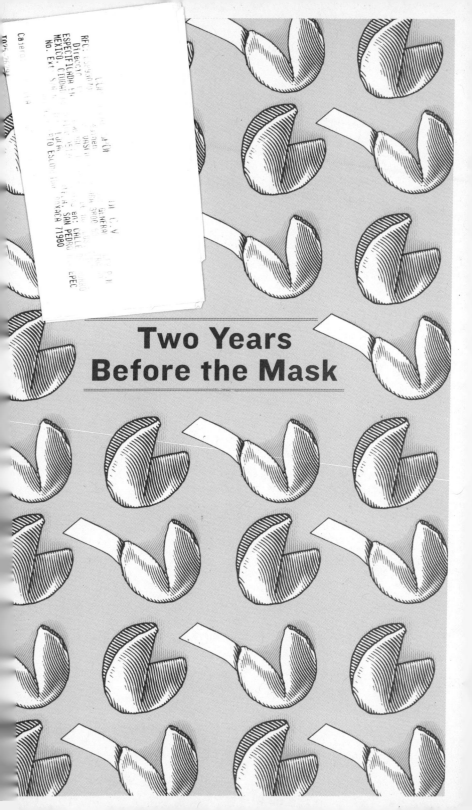

Two Years
Before the Mask

The P-Word

THE BEGINNING OF **2020** was already off to a rough start: Brexit. Megxit. Australia burned down. Kobe Bryant died. So did Takaya the wolf. So did a little bit of your soul after you binge-watched *Tiger King*.

But as terrifying as all that was, it was soon swept aside by the most terrifying threat of modern times. I speak, of course, of the Great Toilet Paper Crisis, the one that had us queuing up at Walmart like it was the chow line at Shawshank.

Then came several months of watching our workmates/ relatives absentmindedly pick their noses on Zoom, along with pretending to home-school children who soon turned feral and now resemble the little kid from *Road Warrior*. (Favourite line stolen from the social media: "Twenty years from now this country will be run by people who were home-schooled by day-drinkers.")

It all became a blur: Plexiglas at the checkout counter. Arrows on the floor. CERB. Sweat pants. Bubbles. Curves. Hearts in windows. COVID hair in your eyes. A cacophony of pots and pans each evening at 7:00 PM. Masks went on and lipstick sales fell off. For some reason, you felt compelled to bake bread (just like Grandma did) and post pictures to Instagram (just like she didn't). Be kind, be calm, be safe—or, if you prefer, hide under the bed.

I mean, not to be a complainer, but given all we were dealing with as the decade began, didn't handing COVID-19 the ball feel just a wee bit like running up the score? Never mind, 2021 would be better. Science had come up with a vaccine that we would all embrace and ... Say what? You've "done your own research?"

Sigh.

The optimist in me says that by the time you read this, the worst of the pandemic will be over—but then, the optimist in me also says I should buy a comb. The pessimist says the aforementioned *Road Warrior* will have turned out to be a documentary, civilization will have crumbled into a dystopian nightmare, and you'll be reading this while lashed to the bumper of an armoured dune buggy en route to the slave market.

Either way, you have to admit the first two years of COVID-19 were quite a wild ride. Think of the next dozen pieces in this book as a trip down memory lane, a diary of our shared adventure you might enjoy (or enjoy skipping past). Without further ado (but with apologies to R.H. Dana, Jr.), I give you Two Years Before the Mask.

Family Time

MARCH 2020

HE SWITCHED OFF THE TV and turned to his wife. "Alice," he began.

"It's Alicia," she said.

"Really? Did you change your first name?"

"No, but I'm thinking of changing my last one. Go on."

"I think it's time that we and our three children . . . "

"Four."

". . . sat down as a family to figure out how we're going to get through this crisis."

"Good idea."

"I mean, are we actually going to have to speak with each other now that our distractions are gone?"

This is the question that gripped him on Saturday while not watching *Hockey Night in Canada*, which had been suspended while the NHL placed its season on hold. He had settled in front of the screen at the regular time, hoping for some blood sport alternative—Aussie rules football, perhaps, or a Democratic primary—but alas, some bright spark at the CBC had decided to stick 2018 PyeongChang Olympic Games figure skating re-runs where *Hockey Night* would usually be. That's like serving quinoa in place of a steak. It's still food, but ... When it comes to televised competitions, the average hockey fan rates figure skating somewhere between *The Bachelor* and *The Great British Bake Off*.

It's not just hockey that's on hold, of course. It's most live sports, suspended for the duration. And it's not just sports either. Theatres, cinemas, bars, restaurants, coffee shops—

many of the places we go, the things that claim our attention, are off-limits for now.

Many people can't even seek the refuge of their usual work-places, whether it's because their jobs are in limbo or because they're now telecommuting from the couch. While it's nice for some to have the option of the latter, it still has its limits: We all like working in our bathrobes, but it's not as much fun when we're barred from the office and we can only do so at home.

Worse, those homes are infested with people in the same predicament—significant others at loose ends, sullen offspring whose idea of spring break hadn't included bonus time with Dad, or, as they liked to call him, "That Guy Who Drives the Car." Right now, they were looking at him with as much enthusiasm as he watched the figure skating.

Nonetheless, he plunged ahead.

"Alice/Alicia," he said, "what are we supposed to do now?"

"Well," she replied, "let's talk about what's important."

He nodded his assent. "Yes, the liquor stores are still open."

She ignored him. "Let's talk about self-isolation."

Again he nodded. "I already told the oldest one to sleep in the back of the truck."

"No," she said. "I mean the self-isolation we live every day of the year. There's not one of us who doesn't go around with our face in a screen all day long."

He couldn't argue with that. Phones, televisions, tablets, computers—even before the pandemic, an Angus Reid Institute survey showed that 22 percent of Canadian children get more than four hours of screen time on a typical weekday.

And that's just the children. The parents might be worse. Teachers say one of the greatest complaints they hear from students is that they feel they come second to their parents' phones. It's as though whatever is on the screen is more important to parents than their own kids.

This isn't new. By 2005, Statistics Canada was already reporting a marked decline in family time over a twenty-year period. And in 2005, parents' electronic tethers didn't leash them to the twenty-four-hour workplace in the way they do today. People didn't call 911 if you took more than five minutes to answer their texts.

"Maybe we should seize this as an opportunity," she said. "Maybe with much of the rest of life on the back burner, we should take this as a time to devote to one another instead of to those things that pull us apart even when we're in the same room. Let's get to know each other again."

She smiled at him the way Henrik Sedin used to smile at Daniel. This brought a tear to his eye, just like when Don Cherry got fired.

He turned to the nearest child. "Let's have some fun together. Jigsaw puzzle? No, go get the Monopoly board, Max."

"Max is the dog," the boy replied. "I'm Kevin."

Mother's Day

MAY 2020

GOOD MORNING, DADS. YOU'RE in trouble.

You forgot which Sunday it is, didn't you? Normally this wouldn't be that big a deal, because your kids would have come home from school with a carefully crafted card in the backpack. Alas, these are not normal times, as we've been told non-stop for the past couple of months. You can't count on your children's teachers to cover your butt on Mother's Day this year, Dad. That means no vases made from mason jars. No Popsicle stick napkin holders. No coffee cup with the words "World's Best Mom" spelled out in glued-on glitter that you'll be vacuuming out of the carpet and/or dog for the next six months. Mother's Day is all up to you, Pa. That's "pa" as in "pandemic." Or "panic."

Breakfast in bed? Too late. Unless you're already buttering the bread, you're toast. Go to the grocery store now and you'll spend twenty minutes staring at the back of another dad's head, six feet away, in what looks like the men's room lineup at a football game.

Can't take her out for brunch either, not this year. The restaurants are closed, though some are doing delivery. Phone right now and your eggs benny might arrive by Wednesday.

Take her to a movie? No. Concert? No. Ballet? Hell no. Maybe present her with a gift, something rare and cherished: toilet paper, or hand sanitizer, or baking supplies ("Say it with flours").

Or maybe you should just whip up your own card with a COVID-themed message from you and the children:

"Be calm, be safe, be kind of nice if you
were to make bacon and eggs for breakfast."

*"If they rammed a Q-tip up my nose to check
our love for you, it would test positive."*
*"To help flatten your curves, we got you an exercise
bike. But not a Peloton. They're expensive."*

You could always absolve yourself of all responsibility by airily declaring, "You're not MY mother"—a wholly accurate, logical argument—but this approach might prove to be less persuasive than it is suicidal.

For here's the deal: This has been a tough year to be a mother. Women who might once have debated the relative merits of full-time employment versus being a stay-at-home mom have discovered that—surprise!—they get to do both at the same time. Some mothers not only get to juggle full-time parenting with full-time careers, they get to be part-time teachers, too. Teachers of subjects they thought they had left behind with their orthodontic devices and Backstreet Boys posters. Great. Why not bring back zits too? Parents who couldn't figure out the tip on a $2 coffee now find themselves wrestling with questions like: "If two trains 300 kilometres apart are travelling toward each other, one with a constant speed of 70 km/h and the other 50 km/h, how long will it take them to meet?" The answer, of course, is "Ask your mother."

This last bit reflects another reality: The lockdown workload is not being shared equally. A survey done for *The New York Times* indicated the burden of homeschooling children during the pandemic has fallen disproportionately on mothers. Household chores, too. The *NYT* isn't the only one noting this gap. Britain's *Guardian* ran a piece headlined "Women's domestic burden just got heavier with the coronavirus," while the *Washington Post* wrote, "Moms will inevitably shoulder extra domestic work during this pandemic."

For those wondering about the train question, the answer is two and a half hours. No word on whether Mom spent the time in the bar car.

Camping Craze

JUNE 2020

STARTLED, SHE DROPPED HER glass, which shattered on the kitchen floor. She stared at me, disbelief in her voice. "What did you say?"

"I'm having an affair," I repeated.

Her shoulders slumped in relief. "Thank goodness," she gasped. "I thought you said you wanted to go camping."

Well, yes, I do, but it seemed prudent to keep that little secret to myself. There are some paths you don't want to go down if you want a relationship to survive. Paths like the one that leads to a campground.

I bring this up now because, in a year in which so many other vacation options have been swept off the table, camping is enjoying a surge in popularity. Or, to be precise, camping preparations have surged. It's still mid-June, so people have yet to try out the gear—sleeping bags, portable stoves, coolers—that has been flying off store shelves like toilet paper was in March. Few of the fifty thousand people who crashed the BC Parks reservation site the moment it opened in May have actually tried to light their first rain-soaked campfire. The green light to travel the province has yet to be given.

In other words, they still think it's going to be fun. No, I want to warn them, it's not. Camping is like running a marathon, where (and here I speak theoretically) the pleasure comes once it's over and the pain has gone.

The only person I knew who adored camping while camping was my dad, who had spent five years sleeping under canvas during the war, and who therefore deemed any excursion not interrupted by the Luftwaffe to be a roaring success. Bugs, biblical rain, Woodstock-quality mud, snot-freezing cold, trench foot, flaming napalm marshmallows that burn through tarpaulins, food that was either burnt to a crisp, raw, or forgotten with the canoe paddles at home—none of this bothered him. His generation was self-reliant and comfortable under the stars and wouldn't starve to death if the grocery store ran out of food.

We're a different breed today. Canada is an overwhelmingly urban country, with more than a third of the population living in just three cities: Vancouver, Toronto, and Montreal. When we talk about "camping," it's an—ahem—big-tent word that takes in everything from luxury glamping at a posh retreat, to a family getaway at Rathtrevor Beach, to getting moose-fighting drunk at a bush party ("Hold my beer, I can take 'im"), or RVing in a Walmart parking lot. Hike into the true, untamed wilderness and you'll find most of the adventurers (in a normal year) come from another country altogether: Germany, the US, Japan, Germany, the Netherlands, Germany, Germany, and Germany.

Modern Canadians prefer a different type of hinterland, one that requires them to bring a credit card. Their idea of camping involves government-groomed roads, assigned campsites, running water, store-bought firewood, pit toilets that smell like something died in them, portable music players, rechargeable blenders, barbecues the size of your first apartment, and a population density that would make Dr. Bonnie just give up and hit the bottle.

There's irony there. Even when seeking solitude, we tend to huddle together. Once, while paddling the Bowron Lakes, my companions and I ended up sharing a campsite with another party who, despite having most of the central Interior at their disposal, set up so close to us that I tripped over their tent peg in the middle of the night. In the morning, one of that tent's occupants, an American woman, said, "I heard a bear last night, but I couldn't find my gun." This raised a series of questions: 1) How did she get her Glock into Canada? 2) What did she expect it would do to a grizzly? 3) What kind of bear takes the Lord's name in vain when it trips over your tent peg?

Having said that, a foray into the forest might be just what we need, given all the angst of the past few locked-down months, our homes getting more and more cramped the longer we shelter in place.

"It would be great to get away from it all," I argued.

"Will you be there?" she asked.

"Yes."

"Then it's not really getting away from it all, is it?" Had to admit, she had a point.

Best Pandemic Ever

JULY 2020

MY CREDIT CARD SLOWLY sank into the murky harbour—deeper, deeper, deeper, and then it was gone. I turned to my wife: "This is the worst pandemic ever."

We were on Fisherman's Wharf and had stopped for ice cream because Victoria has a bylaw that says you must do so on days as glorious as we saw this week.

The problem was that I had dutifully donned a mask while in line, which made it impossible to eat the ice cream when the server handed it to me.

So, brandishing the cone aloft in my right hand—imagine the Statue of Liberty with a fast-melting torch—I used the left, which was already clutching the credit card, to awkwardly pull off my face-covering. That's when the card fell into the water.

Actually, "fell" is inaccurate. What the card really did was take flight, arcing gracefully—and with uncanny accuracy—into the impossibly narrow gap between the wharf and the ice cream shop. It was a perfect shot, nothing but net. Michael Jordan should have asked for my autograph, gushing and blushing like a schoolboy.

"That was fantastic," said my wife. "Now try it with your driver's licence." She was wearing a mask too, which made it hard to tell if she was expressing sarcasm or genuine wonder. Facial cues are so important.

Anyhoo, I blamed all this on the mask, and by extension the pandemic, because the alternative would have been to blame myself.

"The anti-maskers are right," I said. "Also, we should get drunk behind the wheel and blast through red lights, because driving laws impinge on our personal freedom too."

Or maybe that was just virus fatigue talking. That is, shouldn't this be over by now? What do you mean the curve is rising again? When COVID-19 showed up on our doorstep this year, its soggy belongings stuffed in a couple of black plastic garbage bags, it said it would only stay for a couple of months, three tops.

"Just until I get back on my feet," it promised.

Except now it's looking awfully settled-in, isn't it? No sign of leaving any time soon. Its shoes are in the closet, its family photos are on the wall, and positive tests are trending up. We drop hints that it's time for it to go—"Sure would be nice to have a school year, maybe see a concert"—to no avail.

"If it's not going to leave," she whispered to me, watching COVID-19 clip its toenails on the couch, "maybe we should try to appreciate its good side."

So I came up with a list of the pandemic's positive points. Here are my top 10.

10. There will never be a better year to visit Butchart Gardens.
9. For once, your yard looks like Butchart Gardens. Sort of.
8. Life is less cluttered. The treadmill has slowed. No more non-stop racing from home to work to school to soccer game to dinner to piano lesson to meeting to supermarket. Now it's just home to liquor store, home to liquor store, home to liquor . . .
7. No more unwanted hugs. Or restraining orders resulting from unwanted hugs.
6. The latest political scandals seem relatively unimportant. So does everything else that used to turn your face purple.
5. You learned what a "glory hole" was after reading a BC Centre for Disease Control health advisory.
4. More quality time with your loved ones. Or your family.
3. All the cool stuff you didn't know was on Netflix until you had an extra twenty-five hours in your day.

2. We got to forget about hospital parking fees, rush-hour traffic, flight delays, dressing appropriately for work, Pokémon GO, gluten-free as a fad, transit buses that won't stop because they're already full, shaving, the Academy Awards as a political platform, Kim Jong-un, and climate change. Wait, no, don't forget about climate change.

1. It's in the worst of times that the best of us comes out. Most people are being helpful and kind, just like Dr. Bonnie urges. After I deep-sixed my credit card, the couple behind us in line offered to pay for our ice cream. This is the best pandemic ever.

Howling Dog

SEPTEMBER 2020

SOMEWHERE UP THE HILL from my house lives Radar the dog. I don't know precisely where he resides, or what his real name is. I call him Radar after Radar O'Reilly, the company clerk on *M*A*S*H* who could hear incoming helicopters before anyone else. Radar the dog does the same with sirens. Three o'clock in the morning, the whole world as quiet as Oak Bay during *Coronation Street*, and out of nowhere Radar will begin to howl, a low eerie moan like Les Leyne makes when he misses a two-foot putt. Then, faintly in the distance, you'll hear a siren. Ambulance? Police car? Doesn't matter, Radar will already be baying like a banshee by the time the far-off sound registers with you. And once Radar begins the canine chorus, the rest of the neighbourhood dogs will join in, howling and yowling, copycatting (copydogging?) their leader just like politicians during an election campaign.

Radar is not to be confused with Barking Dog, whom long-time readers will remember as my middle-of-the-night tormentor from years past. Barking Dog would shatter the silence with a repeated "Woof! Woof! Woof!" that while unvarying in its content—really, his (or her) messaging was as consistent as Adrian Dix's—was delivered with an irregular cadence, the barking and silence alternating in periods of unpredictable duration.

It was the silences that left you on the edge of the bed, sweating like a U-boat captain waiting for the next depth charge to explode. Coiled there, nerves as frayed and taut as the ready-to-snap waistband of your pandemic-challenged gym shorts, it was hard not to wonder how Barking Dog's owners, whoever they were, could ignore the nightly torture. Were they hard of hearing? Hard of thinking? Perhaps they were dead, lying on the kitchen floor as cold as last night's supper. This last possibility gave me a small measure of joy.

I bore no ill will to Barking Dog himself, though. Nor am I angry with Radar, who is just doing what dogs do. The experts, or at least Google, say dogs howl at sirens due to some ancestral wolf-pack instinct. It's a form of communication, or perhaps eco-location. Me, I'm not so sure. I wonder if Radar hears the siren and goes, "Maybe the cops are pulling over a speeder." But no, the siren wails on and on, which makes the dog wonder if something more serious is happening. Could it be a medical emergency? Radar hopes the guy is OK. A fire? No, if it were, Radar would smell smoke. Maybe a madman is running amok in the neighbourhood. Radar pauses, tries to remember if anyone locked the front door. Oh, if only he had opposable thumbs.

Or maybe it's not the sirens themselves that trigger Radar's howling. Maybe the sirens just wake him up, and the howling comes when all the worries lurking in his subconscious, the ones suppressed during days filled with important hole-digging and the aggressive investigation of his own private parts, drift to the fore. His mind fills with thoughts of COVID. Of back-to-school during COVID. Street crime. Climate change. Cats.

Jeez, Radar wonders, what will happen when the CERB payments run out and the government stops subsidizing wages? Will there be enough people with jobs to carry the load for those without? What will happen to the restaurants when it starts raining on the patios? Maybe he should bury a few bags of Purina, just in case, but then he worries that would make him a hoarder—a bad dog!—a thought that makes him feel shame.

So, feeling uneasy and not knowing what else to do, Radar howls. And the other dogs howl back. Maybe they're getting each other worked up, fuelling the fear. Or maybe they're just trying to reassure one another, or at least let Radar know he's not alone. I'd like to think it's the latter.

"No point in barking at shadows," they're telling him. "We'll all get through this together. This is for now, not forever. Be kind, be calm, be ... squirrel!" And then they all settle down, at least until the next time the sirens wail in the distance. Good dog, Radar.

A Pawcity of Pooches

THE BED GROANED, WHICH is what woke me. In the semi-darkness an antlered figure was silhouetted at the base of the mattress.

I rubbed the sleep from my eyes. "Buck, what are you doing here?"

"Fetching you your paper," he said, though in truth he was reading it, flipping the pages with a cloven hoof.

"Trump's still screaming conspiracy," he reported, "and his crackpot followers still believe him. Do they sell MAGA hats in tinfoil? Somebody could make a fortune."

I sighed, then repeated the question: "Buck, what are you doing?"

"Curling up at your feet," he replied. "It's what we dogs do."

I raised an eyebrow. "Dogs?"

"Woof," he confirmed.

"You're switching species?" I asked.

"Yes," he said. "I'm filling a gap in the market."

I opened my mouth to say something, then paused. In an odd way, Buck made sense. For while Victoria might be over-run with deer—chewing through your garden, razing your roses, stepping in front of your car as oblivious as a guy (OK, me) staring at his phone—it has a shortage of dogs.

Blame the pandemic. People who would normally be snowbirding in Arizona or working in downtown offices now find themselves at home, eager for canine company. Except now there aren't enough dogs to go around. They're like toilet paper and hand sanitizer were last spring. Online, you can find backyard breeders charging thousands for mixed-breed mutts.

The shortage isn't just local.

In Vancouver, the BC SPCA fielded two hundred applications for a single puppy. "Dog adoptions and sales soar during the pandemic," read a headline in the *Washington Post*. The ABC affiliate in San Francisco recently warned of a "Christmas puppy shortage." In Australia, the surge in demand has prompted some shelters to charge adoption fees as high as Aus$1,800. "Fears over dog smuggling as lockdown puppy prices rise by up to 89 per cent," warned the banner over a story by Britain's *Sky News*.

The shortage is in stark contrast to what happened after the financial meltdown of 2008. Back then, the Victoria SPCA saw the number of pets abandoned for financial reasons jump by one-third. The figure was even higher when it came to animals needing medical treatment. Sometimes staff would show up in the morning and find a dog tied to the front railing. Sometimes there would be a box of cats and kittens.

Will we see something similar after COVID-19 restrictions ease? Once free to move around again, some people might decide to ditch their inconvenient pandemic pets.

"Are you sure you're up to being a dog?" I asked Buck.

"Sure," he said. "Lying in the sun. Eating free food. Humping the letter carrier. What's not to like?"

"How about kids using your tail as a tow rope?" I replied. "Collars and leashes. Fleas. The cone of shame. Do you know how much time you have to spend butt-sniffing? It's like being in middle management. Dogs have all sorts of weird habits."

Buck stuck his nose in his private parts, then recoiled. "That's disgusting."

"What about the blind loyalty?" I continued. "It's like being a White House press secretary, only warm-blooded."

His head slumped. "Oh deer."

I kept going. "Let's be honest, you're not great at obedience either. They call you Buck for a reason."

He sniffed. "That's because The Man can't handle my truth."

"The Man," I said, "should be sure he wants a dog, not a temporary distraction."

Doomscrolling

NOVEMBER 2020

DROPPED MY PHONE LIKE it was on fire, tried to hide it under the pillow, but it was too late. She had seen me.

Her eyes narrowed. "What were you looking at?"

"Porn," I blurted. "Terrible stuff. Please accept my heartfelt apologies."

"Stop lying," she replied. "You were doomscrolling." Busted. I hung my head in shame.

Doomscrolling, we are warned, is the newest great threat to our well-being. As addictive as *Better Call Saul*, as destructive as low self-esteem, doomscrolling is defined by *Wikipedia* as "the act of consuming an endless procession of negative online news." Also known as doomsurfing, it's most commonly associated with the compulsion to spend what should be our bedtime hours obsessing over pandemic-related posts. We shiver under our sheets, eyes wide, the gloom relieved only by the pale light from our screens as we twist ourselves into knots with tale after tale of asymptomatic transmission rates, superspreader events, and a future that sounds like *Zombieland III*. For those without a smartphone, you can achieve the same effect by jamming a fork into an electrical outlet and hanging on until your toes start to smoke.

The phenomenon has drawn predictable warnings. "Doomscrolling is slowly eroding your mental health," cautioned *Wired* magazine. "Checking your phone for an extra two hours every night won't stop the apocalypse—but it could stop you from being psychologically prepared for it." *Psychology Today* weighed in, citing studies in the US and Russia that linked rising anxiety levels to the doomscrolling of coronavirus-linked content. The person credited with popularizing the term, Canadian journalist Karen Ho, subsequently began posting nightly reminders urging her Twitter followers to stop doom-scrolling and go to bed.

Good luck with that. In November 2020, news events con-spired to turn doomscrolling into Victorians' favourite hobby, bumping gardening and complaining about bike lanes to second and third place respectively.

Some Islanders sprained their thumbs frantically toggling between the latest numbers from A) the pandemic and B) Trumpistan, where the presidential election ballots were still being counted and fought over like the last sausage sam-ples at Costco. Having two drawn-out crises to fret about had us clutching our phones with one hand and our fluttering hearts with the other.

I shook her awake. "There were 197 new COVID cases in Egypt on Tuesday," I helpfully told her. "Forty-one people in serious or critical condition."

She muttered something about another Canadian being critical if I didn't shut off my phone, but that wasn't going to happen, not with the US presidency in the balance.

"CNN says Parsonsfield County could turn red," I fretted.

"So could I," she replied.

"I didn't know I cared about Parsonsfield County before," I confided. "But now I think it could be the key to all of south-western Maine. Did you know Maine is one of only two states to split its electoral college votes? The other is Nebraska. Speaking of Nebraska, seven COVID-19 cases in the panhandle region were traced to exposures at the Sturgis motorcycle rally in South Dakota, where all but six of sixty-six counties voted for Trump. Do you think he'll try to annex/move to Canada?"

She disappeared after that, presumably to the spare bed-room, though I don't know why she needed a suitcase. Not that I really noticed, having stumbled across a rather alarming account of strange COVID symptoms—rashes, hair loss, a burning sen-sation on the soles of the feet—documented by a researcher at

Indiana University. This, in turn, led me to a story about the Danes slaughtering millions of mink out of fear that they could pass on a mutant strain of the virus, which of course brought me to a piece about Tupperware profits soaring thanks to pandemic shut-ins cooking at home and storing the leftovers. It doesn't take much to disappear down a Facebook rabbit hole.

Speaking of which, did you know a singer named Jaguar Jonze dislocated her shoulder while singing a song called "Rabbit Hole" on live Australian television? It's true. I stumbled across that story too. You can look it up. Or not, which might be the better option unless you want to pass out head-first into your computer keyboard at 4:00 AM, having meandered down a path that somehow led to a conspiracy theory involving one of the lesser-known Von Trapp children.

Or worse, you could make yourself sick relentlessly doom-scrolling through posts about the pandemic.

Last in Line

MARCH 2021

NOW THAT WE'VE DECIDED who's first in line for the vaccine, just one question remains: Who should go last?

That is, after months of jockeying by employee groups trying to position themselves near the front—really, it was like the Porta-Potty queue at Oktoberfest—we have learned who will get priority. The provincial government identified more than 300,000 workers who will receive the inoculation equivalent of the Disneyland fast pass: first responders, K–12 school staff, childcare workers, grocery store employees, posties, bylaw and quarantine officers, manufacturing workers, wholesale/warehousing employees, cross-border transport workers, prison staff, and people who live squeezed together in places such as ski hills.

Fair enough. A solid argument can be made that all those workers are either vital enough or vulnerable enough to warrant bumping them ahead of their age groups. But if that's the case, the reverse should be true, too. There must be certain people who should be shunted not to the front of the line, but to the back. My nominees:

- Telemarketers who call at supper
- Social media influencers
- Street mimes
- The 2011 Boston Bruins
- Anybody caught at a party during the pandemic
- Abusive anti-maskers

- People who wear masks, but under their chins
- That one guy who insists on standing really close while he talks to you, even though you're leaning backward to avoid his COVID breath
- Me

Really, as much as it hurts to say so, I can think of no reason on God's green earth why I should roll up my sleeve before anyone else. As many readers eagerly point out, I am relatively useless.

This was impressed upon me a few summers ago when I happened to be in Kamloops just as the city filled up with thousands of refugees fleeing the forest fires that raged across the Interior that summer. Might as well pitch in with the relief efforts, I thought, and toddled down to Refugee Central to volunteer (fitting myself with an imaginary halo en route).

Alas, upon presenting myself to the volunteer tent I was told thanks but no thanks, they already had all the helpers they needed, or at least all the helpers whose skills were limited to A) typing slowly and B) missing deadlines. Did I have medical training? No. Drive heavy equipment? No. Cook for the masses? No. Don't call us, we'll call you.

As you might expect, this was a tad humbling. It's disconcerting to try to fly to the rescue, only to discover that you are not so much Superman as superfluous. It's unnerving to realize you're not as indispensable as you think, that when the next Great Flood arrives and they're deciding who gets to board the ark, you'll be left dog-paddling in the wake with the performance artists and search engine optimization specialists, watching the farmers and physicians sail away.

The pandemic has, in fact, altered the way many occupations are viewed. According to jobs website Careercast.com, the shipping and transportation industries have become more valued. Behind-the-scenes logisticians who ensure orders are filled have become more essential. Ditto for the network and systems administrators who make it possible to work from home, and the information security analysts who make online conversations and transactions safe. Health care workers, much admired, are expected to remain in demand in the post-pandemic world.

What else qualifies as a good path to follow? Careercast.com periodically produces the *Jobs Rated Report*, which ranks vocations based on income, employment outlook, physical demands, stress, and working environment. The 2019 index declared the top five jobs to be, in order, data scientist, statistician, university professor, occupational therapist, and genetic counsellor.

Newspaper reporter, however, was found all the way down in 222nd place, third from the bottom. The only lower-ranking jobs were logger and, in last place, taxi driver. And here was I thinking I was having a good time.

But I digress. We're supposed to be talking about who should be the caboose on the vaccine train, not who has chosen the wrong track altogether.

Maybe I should just be grateful that a vaccine we were initially told wouldn't come for two years is now here, well ahead of schedule.

(Hand)Shaken

SHOOK SOMEONE'S HAND THIS week. It felt like I cheated on my wife.

Really, after a year and a half of self-conscious elbow bumps and sheepish head nods, it seemed wrong. Ridden with guilt, I confessed when I got home, trying to explain that my handshake kind of happened spontaneously, like that time you accidentally slept with your spouse's best friend. "Baby, it didn't mean anything," I wheedled. "He stuck his hand out and I grabbed it by instinct."

Alas, this explanation did not melt the frost. "Don't tell me it didn't mean anything when you come down with COVID," she said. "Or the flu. Or adenoviral keratoconjunctivitis. Please tell me you were wearing a glove."

I could only hang my head in shame—or perhaps, shamish, with an asterisk.

We are now entering territory where right and wrong aren't black and white. As restrictions ease, we're unsure which pandemic practices to keep and which to chuck away like a disposable mask with a busted elastic. I mean, I torched a car with Alberta licence plates on Friday, but somehow it no longer felt right.

Will we still need Plexiglas? Floor arrows? Hand sanitizer? We're supposed to keep physically distancing, though you may have noticed that for some six feet has already shrunk to the point that you now worry about Buddy lifting your wallet at the checkout counter.

Note that some of the practices we have adopted are not COVID-specific. Some just come down to good hygiene. Proper handwashing, say, or staying home when sick. Dragging your sneezing, coughing carcass to work might once have made you Employee of the Month material ("It's just a cold, boss") but now it's a firing offence. Likewise, don't you dare attempt a dump-and-run at school with your feverish, snotty little Typhoid Mary. Those things are unlikely to change.

Less certain is the future of shared plates of food, everybody plunging their grubby mitts into the same plate of nachos, then licking the salsa and melted cheese off their fingers. Ditto for dunking buffalo wings in the communal blue cheese dip. Does that image leave you: A) horrified or B) hungry?

What about the future of hugs? Even in pre-pandemic times hugging was like patting a stranger's dog, something you didn't want to do without first asking permission, not if you didn't want to lose an arm. Still, people do like physical contact.

Which brings us back to handshakes. CNN quoted an infectious diseases expert as saying he had no qualms about shaking hands with a vaccinated person but wouldn't do so with those whose status was unknown. What really made him wary was not so much the physical contact but getting near enough to suck in their COVID-laden breath. Of course, he was only speaking about the danger of contracting COVID-19, not other diseases. A 2013 story in the *Atlantic* said up to eighty per cent of all infections are transmitted by hand and "it would be more sanitary to intertwine almost any other part of our bodies, apart from our lips or genitals."

OK, but shaking hands is something built into our cultural DNA. It conveys respect, good manners, trust. "We didn't need to sign a contract, we shook hands," we say. A firm shake is taken as a sign of strong character, whereas a limp one signals a limp personality and a crushing one is a red flag for doofusness (Donald Trump used handshakes as a psychological weapon, subjecting other world leaders to a vise-like grip, then hanging on like a bad case of the flu). It is considered the height of sportsmanship for hockey players who have spent seven games attempting to murder one another to line up for handshakes at the end of a playoff series—though some youth sports have, thanks to COVID-19, substituted a socially distanced walk-by, which frankly comes across as a bit passive aggressive, more cat than dog.

That leads to the next question: What's the alternative to the handshake? Fist bumps are a bit too bro. Touching elbows seems contrived (and aren't those the same elbows we sneeze into?). Some suggest bowing while putting your hand over your heart, but that seems a tad intimate if all you're trying to do is buy car insurance. Toe-to-toe tapping? Barf. A simple wave? Perhaps, but potentially fatal if you flash a gang sign by mistake.

For now, I remain shaken by my handshake.

Corporate Caring

JULY 2021

I GOT A MESSAGE FROM Facebook this morning.

"Jack," it began, "we care about you and the memories that you share." Enclosed, thoughtfully, was a photo I had posted four years previously. Would I like to make it public again? Now, a cynic might have replied, "Of course you care. Were it not for me and the memories I share, Facebook wouldn't have seen its revenue grow 48 percent to $26.2 billion US in the first three months of this year." But I, of course, am not a cynic. I took the message for what it really was—a pleasantly surprising act of kindness by a transnational corporate behemoth with my best interests at heart.

So I sent a response: "Thanks for caring about my feelings. As the pandemic stretches into a second summer, emptying the calendar of the events with which we normally fill our days, I realize my existence is a hollow shell, devoid of purpose, passion, and meaning. Strip away the polite facade, remove the inconsequential trivia with which we clutter our minds, and the vacuum is ineluctably filled with the great, overwhelming, unanswerable questions about the human condition and life itself. On the other hand, my tomato plants are coming up nicely. Say hi to Zuckerberg!" It's nice to have friends with whom you can express yourself freely.

Facebook is not my only distant confidante, though. I get earnest check-ins from a whole range of interests who, even while conducting business from places thousands of kilometres away, are eager to ensure I'm OK. "Jack, we hope you are doing well in these unprecedented times," they write. "You know what would make you feel better? A new truck." There is an entire community of such helpers out there. It takes a village.

Not that this sort of corporate caring is new. Twenty years ago, I began getting Christmas cards from an Illinois-based manufacturer of printing-related equipment. I don't know how our relationship began, as I had absolutely nothing to do with the press at the newspaper. Nonetheless, it was comforting to know that while others would drift in and out of my life, I could at least count on my old pals in Illinois, whose cards would arrive with the dependable timing of one of the company's own three-stage compensating stackers.

I would also get personal Christmas greetings from politicians I had never met, though none went as far as Paul Martin, who, as federal Liberal leader in 2002, took time out of his busy schedule to send a card to a dead golden retriever from Saanich that had somehow made it onto the party's membership list. The dog also received two invitations from the BC Young Liberals to attend functions at the University of Victoria, a gracious gesture given that Gregg (that was the retriever's name) wasn't even an alumnus.

These days see fewer holiday greetings but an absolute avalanche of communications from far-off correspondents—corporations, charities, advocacy groups—who, while embarrassingly anonymous to me, nonetheless consider themselves familiar enough to use my first name. Sometimes they use an exclamation point—"Jack!"—to show how excited they are to have me in their lives.

I raise all this now because I just phoned a far-off service provider, only to be answered by a recording: "Your call is important to us. Please stay on the line."

So I stayed on the line. And stayed. Answered some emails. Watched *The Irishman* on Netflix—twice. Stayed some more.

Then, while waiting, I discovered that mine was not an isolated case. I stumbled across a *Business Wire* story about a survey of call centres, one that found hold times had increased 50 percent since the start of the pandemic. Just over half of all callers had waited more than thirty minutes to get a response.

"Good heavens," I thought. "Here are these poor people who care about me so much but who are unable to answer my call. They must be beside themselves with worry. Maybe I should message them on Facebook, let them know I'm all right."

Maybe we should all write our far-off connections when put on hold like that, if only to assure them that we care about them just as much as they care about us.

Thanksgiving

OCTOBER 2021

S HE STOPPED ME AT the door: "Vaccine card, please."

I paused. "Are you sure that's necessary?"

She smiled blandly, but didn't move aside. "I think it is."

Defeated, I showed her the image on my phone—though I couldn't help pointing out the obvious. "You know this is our house, right?"

"Yes," she replied.

"And you remember that you and I are married?" I asked.

"Of course," she said. "Now, do you have any photo ID?"

"Phot...?"

"Cough? Headache? Fever? Have you or anyone in your household travelled outside Canada in the past two weeks?"

"You are my household," I said. "And you just sent me to the store for cranberry sauce."

"Thanks for that," she said. "Put it in the kitchen. Just follow the arrows."

I peered over her shoulder. "Arrows?"

"Six feet!" she barked, so I dutifully scuttled back.

Jeez, I thought, Thanksgiving dinner is going to be different this year. All this awkwardness about who is allowed in whose home, whether it's polite to ask about vaccine status, and should the rapid test kit go to the left of the salad fork or beside the napkin.

What we forget is that last Thanksgiving there was no turkey dinner at all, or at least nobody was buying a twenty-pounder. "Small bubbles only," we were told. "Stick to your safe six." (Remember that?) In lieu of communal feasts, some creative Victorians swapped dishes. They'd leave them on one another's porches, then ring the doorbell and flee as though what they'd just dropped off was a flaming bag of dog crap, not a steaming bowl of Brussels sprouts. As much as we might moan about today's restrictions, we're living in a veritable mosh pit relative to last year's isolation.

Another thing we forget about at Thanksgiving? Giving thanks.

Regular readers of my columns might recognize this is something I like to do each year at this time: step back, take stock, count my blessings—then jealously compare them with those of others. This time, I was appalled to find I had seven fewer blessings than my brother-in-law Eric. Ticked me right off. My other brother-in-law, Al, shot his age on the golf course this year—twice!—yet I didn't even get a round in. The BC Ferries Wi-Fi crapped out, forcing me to take stress leave. I mean, my car doesn't even have a back-up camera. It might as well be a Model T.

We've been over this before, God. As an older Canadian man like myself, you know there are things to which I am entitled: clean water, paved roads, whatever I want to eat whenever I want to eat it, Bluetooth headphones, a two-car garage that isn't big enough, a television the size of that garage's door, at least six Sportsnet channels, air conditioning in summer, heated floors in winter, and a dog that gets better health care than most mothers in the developing world.

Yet, thanks to the pandemic, the past couple of years have seen some slippage. Stores ran short of hand sanitizer, which I didn't know I wanted until I couldn't have any. I had to learn about masks, vaccines, and patiently waiting my turn, just like other, less important Canadians. I had tickets to see the Rolling Stones in Vancouver and David Sedaris in Victoria, but they cancelled. There's nothing left to watch on Netflix. Is this a test, God? What's next, a plague of locusts?

Never mind. Mustn't grumble. Better to take the high road and express gratitude for the good things that have happened in the past year. Here goes:

- I am thankful that scientists found a way to lessen the chance of contracting COVID-19. Added bonus: Thanks to Ivermectin, I am worm-free.

- I am grateful for the self-pity of those who protest outside hospitals, for otherwise they might feel overwhelmed by guilt. Yes, God, that's sarcasm.
- I am grateful that I haven't felt compelled to mention Donald You-Know-Who since January. I would be super thankful, though, if the no-shirt, painted-face, horned-fur-hat Capitol Hill insurrection guy became this year's go-to Halloween costume.
- I am grateful that for the first time, Canada has topped the annual Best Countries Report's rankings of 78 nations.
- I am somewhat less grateful that a separate analysis, the United Nations' Human Development Index, only rated Canada the sixteenth best country out of 189. Sixteenth out of 189 might be fine for one of those countries where children in sweatshops make the clothes we throw away after three washes, but here in the Great Whine North, where our sense of entitlement is only slightly smaller than our fervent belief that we are hard done by, we expect a little better.
- I am thankful that should I find sixteenth-ranked Canada too burdensome, I am free to move to any of the war- and famine-stricken countries on the bottom of the list. I'll try not to hit my butt with the door on the way out.
- I am grateful for Dr. Bonnie Henry and her mantra of "be kind, be calm, be safe."
- I am glad Dr. Bonnie didn't see me climb atop a rickety chair, wild-eyed and cursing, to take out a 3:00 AM malfunctioning smoke detector with a garden rake.
- I am grateful she suggested small gatherings for Thanksgiving dinner, for that means more stuffing, turkey, and gravy for me.
- I am grateful for Pepto Bismol.
- I am grateful for the chance to see that while things are not that great, neither are they—for most of us—that bad. To quote Kentucky poet Kat Savage: "Life is

simply a mix of mayhem and magnolias, so embrace this gentle riot and gather flowers along the way."

Bring On the Mutant Zombies

DECEMBER 2021

THAT'S IT?

That's all you've got? Fire-hose rain, farm-eating floods, a succession of hellacious storms lining up to tag-team us—pow, pow, pow!—like the bad guys on Saturday night wrestling?

I mean, if you're going to go all *Hunger Games* on us, you're going to have to do better than that. We've seen highways wash out like Trump in a Women's Studies program and bridges collapse like the Green Party in the last federal election, but we're still on our feet—wobbly for sure, but we haven't fallen on our knees. So bring it on, hit us with another storm and then another one after that, except maybe throw in some bloodthirsty mutant zombies, acid fog, and a toilet paper shortage too.

It's late 2021. We're staggering toward our second COVID Christmas and it has been soul-suckingly sloppy, gloomier than a Goth, more miserable than a Canucks fan, more destructive than social media. Santa Claus bailed out of his own parade and was replaced by Aquaman. Port Renfrew had more than a thousand millimetres of rain in November, enough to drown a weatherman, not that I'm necessarily suggesting anything. What is the Roto-Rooter man doing in the basement? It appears to be the backstroke.

It has been so bad that—get this—the rest of the country feels sorry for us. This is unnerving. Usually when the West Coast is hit with wild weather, other Canadians ask, "What's wrong?" and we reply that we were absolutely buried in half an inch of snow, which makes them smirk and ask if we need grief counsellors or just a glass of warm milk.

A few years ago, I went on a Toronto radio show where the host struggled to contain herself as I described one of Victoria's infrequent brushes with Real Canadian Winter. "Say it again," she urged. "Tell me how minus six was 'brutally cold.'" These might not have been her exact words. It was hard to tell over the sound of her slapping her knee.

I tried explaining, again, that Victoria measures winter like dog years, and you have to multiply everything—snow, freezing temperatures, Prozac prescriptions—by seven to get the true impact, but she cut me off. "Suck it up like the rest of us," she said.

Suck it up? Victorians don't pay $87.10 for car and driver and sink their life's savings into a two-bedroom glorified storage shed only to be told to "suck it up."

No, that sort of nonsense belongs to lesser parts of Canada, the bits that God still loves but just not as much as those where board shorts are considered winter wear and minus 30 is the sale price. Our tiny, pink, uncalloused hands are built to hold umbrellas, not snow shovels.

At least, that's the image we project: Victoria, where the only flakes we see are the ones we elect. Nobody here even owns a shovel or ice scraper, because it never snows, except for every single winter, which is when the cookie sheets and credit cards get pressed into service.

That's the natural order of things. We all have our roles to play in the Great Canadian Dramedy, and ours is to go full-on Three Stooges for the entertainment of the rest of the country when winter pays a visit. Other Canadians just pray that the next time Vancouver Island is on the television, the screen will show post-earthquake looters turning what remains of the City of Gardens into a scene from *Lord of the Flies*. We don't expect people from the land of gas-line antifreeze and square tires to fret about our weather. Having just, for the millionth time, smacked their frozen knuckles on the grille of the truck while unplugging a stubborn block heater cord, they are not likely to weep for wimps who need stress leave when their socks get wet.

Except this time, people from the other side of the Rockies are showing genuine sympathy. Trudeau came to BC to check out the damage and didn't even surf. Saskatchewan sent sand-bagging machines. The CBC reported that when an Alberta restoration company asked for people to help with the clean-up in BC, some volunteered to come from other parts of the country to work for free. An Alberta Christian group drove a massive disaster-response trailer to the Fraser Valley. Not long ago, Albertans were so mad at us that they banished BC wine from their liquor stores and threatened to turn off the oil taps. Now they're acting like the physician who, after wincing at your test results, gently asks about your bucket list. It would be more reassuring if, when Albertans talked about burying the hatchet, they meant in our heads, just like in the good old days.

Or maybe their concern just means the shared pandemic pain has brought our bickering family together. Maybe those broken supply chains have proven how interdependent we are. Maybe there's a sense that after almost two years of lockdowns, travel bans, home-schooling, day-drinking, anti-vaxxers, "we can't hear you" Zoom calls, bubbles, Plexiglas, masks, and 911 calls to narc out travellers with Alberta licence plates (don't you feel bad about that now?), to subject us to a series of meteorological muggings worthy of their own state of emergency smells just a tad like overkill, like being run over by a bus after being struck by lightning. And oh, just to top it all off, now we have the latest COVID-19 variant to worry about. What's next? The winged monkeys from *The Wizard of Oz*?

Never mind. The water might be up to BC's knees, but we're still on our feet. Keep going.

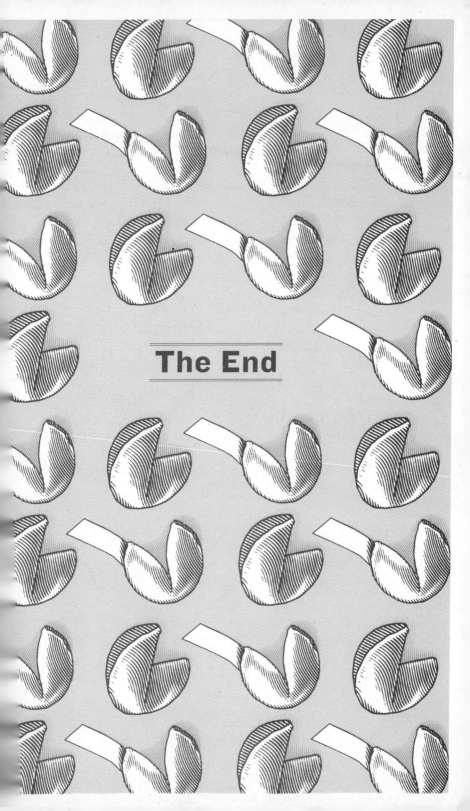

The End

The End

PART ONE

GAWDA CODE. RUNNING NOSE, bleary eyes, sandpaper throat, sinuses more painful than a schoolgirl's crush on Justin Bieber. Can't just be a cold. Must be Creutzfeldt-Jakob disease, the human variant of mad cow. I knew I shouldn't have eaten British processed meat in the 1980s.

I stagger into the living room, where my wife is reading a book. "I'm dying."

"Good luck with that," she says, eyes never straying from the page. She ran the whole Victoria marathon while nursing the same cold that I have, whereas I set a personal best playing Wordscapes on my phone. I'm feeling pretty proud of myself, or at least I would be were I not dying.

"What if I get famous?" I ask her.

"Pardon?"

"What if I get famous after I die, like Stieg Larsson?"

This gives her cause for pause, a reason to put down her copy of Larsson's *The Girl with the Dragon Tattoo*. It's a big, 841-page bug-killer of a book, still popular all these years later. "Do you have an unpublished manuscript I don't know about?" she asks.

Good point. Swedish author Larsson had three of them languishing on an IKEA shelf. He never did get to see them in print, was just fifty years old in 2004 when his heart packed it in, five months before *Dragon Tattoo* was published. All three crime novels in his Millennium Trilogy went on to become bestsellers, with 80 million copies sold by 2015. They comprised the hottest literary series since J.K. Rowling wrote *Harry Potter and the Magical Merchandising Machine*. Except where Rowling is covered in literary laurels, Larsson is pushing up daisies. Sucks to be Stieg.

Larsson, the suitably unwealthy editor of an anti-fascist magazine while alive, generated a fortune worth in the tens of millions after his death. He also left behind a very public, very nasty feud between the woman he lived with for thirty-two years and his blood relations who, because Swedish law didn't recognize common-law marriages, collected all the kronor.

"Please don't squabble over my fortune," I implored my wife.

"I get the signed Guy Lafleur puck," she replied. "Your sisters can fight over the ice-fishing auger."

Of course, Larsson was not the first writer to become famous only after death.

Poet Emily Dickinson was all but unpublished prior to keeling over. Ditto for Edgar Allen Poe, Henry David Thoreau, and Sylvia Plath. John Keats barely gave the public a chance to know his stuff, croaking at age twenty-five. When Franz Kafka died at forty, he left instructions for his best friend, Max Brod, to burn his works unread; instead, Brod had them published. Had Brod not done so, millions of wispy-whiskered, scarf-draped film students would have been denied the word "Kafkaesque" and would have been forced to use the more prosaic "I'm a pretentious knob" instead.

The music world is full of people who become well known in life but absolutely boffo in death. Jim Croce slogged away without reward for years, even going back to construction just before finally finding success in 1972, only to die in a plane crash a year later. Buddy Holly, plane crash. Lynyrd Skynrd, plane crash.

American singer Eva Cassidy died at age thirty-three in 1996, four years before her rendition of "Somewhere Over The Rainbow" made her an overnight sensation. Her posthumously released recordings sold more than 8 million copies, including a version of "What a Wonderful World" that topped the UK charts. (Oddly enough, Hawaii's Israel "Brudda Iz" Kamakawiwo'ole enjoyed posthumous stardom with a ukulele medley of both "Rainbow" and "Wonderful World" several years after his death.)

Starving artists in general are famous for, well, starving before fame. Vincent van Gogh sold only a single painting, *The Red Vineyard*, before his death. Paul Gauguin, with whom Van Gogh quarrelled on the day the Dutchman severed his ear ("I SAID, VINCENT, WHY DID YOU CUT OFF YOUR … oh, never mind") was also a commercial flop. "I am now down and out, defeated by poverty," Gauguin wrote not long before dying, reportedly of syphilis.

Or maybe it was a cold.

The End

PART TWO

THE GOOD NEWS, UPON returning home from a holiday, is that it wasn't hard to find the raw hamburger that I took out of the freezer just before the hot weather arrived.

"That's all right, I'll clean it up," she said, though with her voice muffled by the hazmat suit, it sounded like "I'm going to feed this to you in your sleep."

Well, no, what she really said was that it might have been she who left the meat on the counter. I could have disabused her of this notion, admitted that the fault was mine, but what actually came out of my mouth was "I forgive you."

Jack Knox is big-hearted that way. He's also lousy at admitting blame, which came to mind when reading the obituary of a Salt Lake City man named Val Patterson, who while terminally ill wrote his own death notice, and whose cheerful honesty has caused it to go viral.

The fifty-nine-year-old revealed some indiscretions, from kicking rocks into Old Faithful to earning bans from Disneyland and SeaWorld. "As it turns out, I AM the guy who stole the safe from the Motor View Drive Inn in June 1971," he wrote.

Patterson confessed that he only received his PhD through a clerical error at the University of Utah, that he didn't even have an undergraduate degree—not that it held him back.

"For all of the electronic engineers I have worked with, I'm sorry, but you have to admit my designs always worked very well, and were well engineered, and I always made you laugh at work."

It isn't unheard of for people to wait until death before revealing private bits of their life or unburdening themselves while preparing to meet their maker. Approaching the end in

1993, Britain's Christian Spurling declared that the famous 1934 "surgeon's photo" of the Loch Ness monster—the grainy black-and-white of a longnecked creature with a horse-like head—was a hoax in which he had had a hand.

Just before his death in 1985, musician Julian Altman told his wife he had stolen Polish violinist Bronislaw Huberman's Stradivarius from Carnegie Hall half a century earlier. His wife got insurer Lloyd's of London to pay her a $263,000 finder's fee for the return of the pilfered fiddle, which Altman had played in public for decades.

Prior to expiring in 2020, a Boston man revealed to his wife of almost forty years that not only was he guilty of a half-century-old crime, making off with $215,000 while working as bank teller in Cleveland in 1969, but he had adopted a new identity before meeting her. An Associated Press story described the seventy-one-year-old as a "gentle soul" whose crime might have been inspired by the 1969 movie *The Thomas Crown Affair*, which was about an executive who treated a bank heist as a game.

But, as in comedy, timing is everything when it comes to deathbed confessions. In 2005, an elderly Brit who thought he was dying revealed to his wife that he had slept with her best friend years earlier. To his surprise, he rallied from his illness—only to be stabbed to death by his wife in 2010 as they quarrelled about his affair.

This is all of little help to those of us who might feel weighed down by guilt while in good health. I decided to come clean about the raw hamburger, albeit while framing my confession in a positive way: "The good news is that I didn't sleep with your best friend like that British guy."

She wasn't as forgiving as one might have hoped, a failing I pointed out while preparing to sleep on the couch.

"At least I didn't wait until I was on my deathbed," I said.

"Don't be so sure of that," she replied.

The End

PART THREE

BEFORE HE SLIPPED AWAY, this is what Hornby Island's Billy Little said he wanted written on his tombstone:

BILLY LITTLE

POET

HYDRO IS TOO EXPENSIVE

That wish was tacked on to his self-penned obituary, which read:

> After decades of passion, dedication to world peace and justice, powerful friendships, recognition, being loved undeservedly by extraordinary women, a close and powerful relationship with a strong, handsome, capable, thoughtful son Matt, a never-ending stream of amusing ideas, affections shared with a wide range of creative men and women, a long residence in the paradisical landscape of Hornby Island, success after success in the book trade, fabulous meals, unmeasurable inebriation, dancing beyond exhaustion, satori after satori, Billy Little regrets he's unable to schmooze today. In lieu of flowers please send a humongous donation to the War Resisters League.

Now that, dear reader, is an obituary. That is how, with good humour and panache, we should all have the courage to go out.

Alas, many obituaries resemble Wikipedia entries, offering more about what the subjects did than who they were. The worst ones veer between sanitized and mawkish, leaving us with a Disneyfied deceased: "He had a big heart, but undersized lungs."

It doesn't have to be that way. In her book *The Dead Beat*, Marilyn Johnson noted that North American obits tend to celebrate the extraordinary qualities of ordinary people, while the British are more irreverent, painting a fuller picture of the departed. For some fascinating final notices, read *Deadlines: Obits of Memorable British Columbians* by Victoria's Tom Hawthorn, who, like Jesus, is terrific at bringing the dead to life.

In that spirit was this 2003 obit opening by *Times Colonist* reporter Richard Watts: "Rude and foul-mouthed, Dr. Jim Buchan was possibly the most brilliant physician and keenest mind to ever live on Salt Spring Island. In a community that prides itself on its acceptance of eccentrics, Buchan stood out as an eccentric who sometimes pushed even Salt Spring tolerance too far. At the same time, nobody seems to doubt his intelligence, professional ability, generosity of spirit, or his moral decency." Sounded like Dr. House before there was a Dr. House.

Good obits can say a lot with a little: "Agate, population 70, is one of those towns that people describe as 'blink and you'll miss it,'" wrote the *Denver Post*. "Lois A. Engel loved living in the blink." The *Atlanta Journal-Constitution* captured artist and prankster Carole Connelly in a single telling detail: "If her husband dozed off early, she handed out washable markers to her children to decorate him while he slept." One of my all-time favourite obits ran in the *New York Times*: "Selma Koch, a Manhattan store owner who earned a national reputation by helping women find the right bra size, mostly through a discerning glance and never with a tape measure, died Thursday in New York. She was 95 and a 34B."

And jeez, if you want to read one of the most rollicking send-offs ever, Google the obit for Renay Mandel Corren that ran in the December 15, 2021, edition of the *Fayetteville Observer* newspaper in North Carolina. "A plus-sized Jewish lady redneck died in El Paso on Saturday," it begins. "Of itself hardly news, or good news if you're the type that subscribes to the notion that anybody not named you dying in El Paso, Texas, is good news."

I also liked the obituary placed in the *Times Colonist* by cartoonist Adrian Raeside after the death of his father. Adrian asked that mourners, in lieu of flowers, send single-malt scotch and Cuban cigars. They did.

This all leads to an uncomfortable question. "What would your obituary say if you died today?" my friend Erin Glazier once asked, inspired by a candid, funny-but-painful death notice in the *Times Colonist*. If you were run over by a steamroller tomorrow, how would your death notice read? ("He was large in life, flat in death.") Would your obit be like that of Billy Little, the poet and activist, or just an underwhelming au revoir?

Writing your own obituary can be a pretty depressing exercise, even if you're not dead. So far, mine goes something like this: "He had a good dog." Whatever happened to the greatness I was going to achieve? Apparently it got back-burnered while I was watching Hockeyfights.com. Perhaps it would be more realistic to aim for simple decency instead, but even that goal is easily forgotten as we trundle along on the treadmill. I have toyed with lying in my obit ("After parting with Mother Teresa, Jack invented Velcro") but fear getting caught posthumously, tarnishing my reputation.

Of course, the best way to control what is written is to create your own legacy while there is still time. They say it was a premature obituary that rattled Alfred Nobel into changing the way he would be remembered. In 1888, a French newspaper mistakenly reported the death of the inventor of dynamite with a story that read "Dr. Alfred Nobel, who became rich by finding ways to kill more people faster than ever before, died yesterday." Nobel's response was to leave most of his money to what would become the Nobel Prizes.

Unfortunately, most of us don't get this kind of Ghost of Christmas Future kick-start. Instead, we live lives of deferred awesomeness, waiting to put our stamp on the world until after the mortgage is paid, or the kids are out of school, or the second coat of paint is on the deck. I totally plan to become awesome— as soon as I get caught up on the third season of *Ted Lasso*. Until then, the eulogy might be a little thin.

Which brings us back to Erin's question: "What would your obituary say if you died today?" I thought for a minute, then typed: "Jack is dead. Funeral Friday. Bicycle for sale, $200 OBO."

Acknowledgements

A S A YOUNG NEWSPAPER reporter, I once covered what turned
into a raucous confrontation outside a union office. Eager
to file by deadline, I raced to a neighbouring McDonald's,
vaulted the counter and demanded "Press! Get me a phone!"
The kid at the counter complied, providing me not only with the
telephone in the manager's office, but a coffee and side of fries.

Quite pleased with myself, I told my city editor what I had
done, assuming that he, too, would be impressed. Instead, there
was silence from the other end of the phone, followed by what
might have been the sound of a man repeatedly slamming his forehead against a desk. Then I heard him say, "Never do that again."

It was the first time I remember disappointing an editor. It
was far from the last. Dreadfully ungracious of me, considering
how much help I have had from editors and other newspaper
colleagues—the ink-stained wretches to whom this book is dedi-
cated—over the past 45 years. I'm particularly grateful to the
dyspeptic Dave Obee, the unreasonably serene Bryna Hallam,
the always-enthusiastic Pat Coppard and everyone else who has
propped me up at the Victoria *Times Colonist*, where for a quarter century I have written the column that provided much of the
material in this book. They are very good at what they do—and
routinely give more than they get in return—because of their
belief in the role of local journalism. I hope you believe in it, too.

This is the fourth book I have done with the people at
Heritage House, and I pray they are as happy with me as I am
with them. (It can be hard to tell; book people are unnervingly
polite.) Hats off to Rodger Touchie, Lara Kordic, Nandini Thaker,
Jacqui Thomas, Monica Miller, Setareh Ashrafologhalai, Kimiko

Fraser, and John Walls. As an editor, Lesley Cameron made me look better than I am and occasionally saved me from myself.

Thanks to my pal Lindsay Kines for helping me decide what to cut from this book. Really, if you thought some of the stories you just read were weak, you should see the lame stuff that got left out.

As always, I am most grateful for the unwavering support of my long-suffering wife Lucille, whose judgment is seriously flawed.

Eric Glazier

JACK KNOX is the author of three bestselling books, *Hard Knox: Musings from the Edge of Canada*, *Opportunity Knox: Twenty Years of Award-Losing Humour Writing* (both long-listed for the Leacock Medal for Humour), and *On the Rocks with Jack Knox: Islanders I Will Never Forget*. All of his books are based on his popular column in the Victoria *Times Colonist*. Women adore him. Men want to be him. His hobbies include cycling, playing in a rock 'n' roll band, being awesome, and self-delusion.